THE CURE FOR HUMAN TROUBLES

THE CURE
FOR HUMAN TROUBLES

A STATEMENT OF THE CHRISTIAN
MESSAGE IN MODERN TERMS

by

W. MONTGOMERY WATT

with a Foreword by
the Right Reverend Kenneth C. H. Warner
Bishop of Edinburgh

LONDON
S·P·C·K
1959

First published in 1959
by S.P.C.K.
Holy Trinity Church, Marylebone Road,
London, N.W.1

Printed in Great Britain by
Billing and Sons, Ltd., Guildford and London

CONTENTS

FOREWORD

IN THE fourth section of this book, the author has given us an illuminating account of the way in which the meaning of words in different languages and the modes of thought of different peoples, led to misunderstanding and so-called heresies, and to consequent divisions in Christendom.

In the circumstances of to-day, however far removed from the temper and outlook of the early centuries of Christianity, a similar danger exists and is having similar results. Within the circle of those who profess and call themselves Christians, there are the unhappy divisions to which Dr Watt refers, many of which are due not to genuine theological differences but to different ways of expressing the same thing.

Still more is this true in the relation between the Christian Church and the world of modern thought. There is a profound difference of language and mode of thought between them. Yet we are largely concerned with and talking about the same things.

Here is a courageous and scholarly contribution to the task of interpretation. The great Christian dogmas are described in terms of modern psychology, and the concepts of Jung and his disciples are shown to find their fulfilment in the person and work of Jesus Christ.

For those of us who have been brought up in the Christian tradition, it may be difficult to think and express ourselves in new terms. "O Lamb of God that takest away the sin of the World" is more meaningful to us than the assertion that "Jesus was deliberately living out an archetypal synthesis" (Section 2, Ch. 3). But the contrary is true for those trained in a different school of thought.

I commend this book to both parties. It will, I believe, help those of modern and scientific outlook to understand the relevance of the claim of Christ in every age and under all modes of thought and language. It will also assist those accustomed to the more traditional expressions of Christian belief to understand how it is possible to re-interpret these in modern terms and yet remain orthodox.

KENNETH EDENBURGEN :

INTRODUCTION

THIS BOOK is in intention completely orthodox. However revolutionary some of its statements may appear at first sight, their aim is simply to translate into terms of modern thought the faith once for all delivered to the saints, as it is contained in the New Testament and safeguarded by the oecumenical creeds of the Church. If this book achieves its aim, it will lead men back to orthodoxy, not away from it—back to a whole-hearted acceptance of the New Testament, the creeds, and the authority of the Church. Thus its attitude cannot properly be called modernistic or even liberal.

In considering the application of the Christian message to modern problems I have not discussed the application to matters of personal relationship, since these belong to all ages, but have confined myself to what may be called the social and communal sins that are proving specially troublesome in our time. This limitation of the discussions in the third chapter does not mean that the application of the "cure" to personal relationships is denied, but only that it is taken for granted.

1

THE SOURCE OF OUR TROUBLES

I WHAT IS WRONG WITH THE WORLD?

Preliminary description

IT IS not necessary at the middle of the twentieth century to labour the point that there is something seriously wrong with the world. Nevertheless, it is worth while spending a little time on a survey of the outstanding features of the troubles of mankind.

In the minds of many people the chief trouble is undoubtedly the threat of war, war of such a kind that the whole fabric of civilized life may be disrupted. Nobody knows, of course, even if atomic war should come, just how destructive it would be. Would the destruction be so vast that the cultural level of those who survived bombs and famine might be reduced to approximately that of the Dark Ages, or of neolithic times? Or would it be merely a temporary dislocation from which the world might recover in twenty or thirty years? We cannot say. Probably men's fears make them exaggerate the material destruction and loss of life, just as before the second World War it was thought that the casualties would be far higher than in fact they were. Even if this is so, however, an atomic war would bring widespread death and destruction, and perhaps also sufferings worse than death.

The threat of atomic war is bad enough in itself; yet behind it there appears an even greater evil, the domination of human wills by seemingly demonic forces. The great majority of mankind are terrified at the prospect of atomic war and crave for peace. It is by no means certain, however, that this almost universal longing will be effective. Mankind is also full of suspicion and distrust, of prejudice and hatred. Each people, or nation, or national minority, seeks its own interests without much concern for those of others, and as a result all feel insecure. A few ambitious men, in reckless lust for power, might so sway the emotions and passions of the masses that the conditions for peace were forgotten and courses adopted which made war inevitable. Indeed, it is not even necessary to suppose irresponsible ambitions. Well-intentioned men, led astray by prejudice, suspicion, and the feeling of insecurity, might, while believing that they were promoting human welfare, plunge the world into war. In view of such a possibility there is justification for speaking about "demonic forces", at least in a metaphorical sense.

When one turns from international affairs to the internal politics of each country something similar is to be seen. The various groups and subdivisions of the people of a country generally distrust and often hate one another. Those who have the opportunity exploit other groups. Class hatred and class war are rife. Those whose share of the national wealth is increasing are not satisfied but try to obtain still more. Those whose share of the national wealth is decreasing are often embittered. The various classes and groups lack the sense of being together, of having complementary functions in the business of living. In these respects the state of affairs in some countries is better than in others; but none is perfect. In general, too, the situation seems to be deteriorating. In the case of the chief belligerents the second World War halted the process temporarily, but the "cold war" rather speeds it up.

Another unsatisfactory feature of the social life of our time is the decline in the quality of individual or personal relationships. Men are ceasing to be full persons and are becoming parts of a mass. It is machines which have made the masses, and something of the spirit of the machine has insinuated itself into our personal relationships. We meet so many people and are in such a hurry that we often forget that the bus conductor, the shop assistant, even the teacher of our children, are not just cogs in a machine. The growth of such impersonal relations between persons is perhaps inevitable in a society organized as ours is; yet it is a bad tendency, to be resisted and counteracted as far as possible.

At the same time, because of the importance of the masses in our national life, there is a danger that standards of taste will be lowered, the standards of the masses replacing those of the élite. In so far as the élite has become cut off from the rest of the community this would be no great loss. The élite, however, is not entirely isolated, and there is therefore a degree of loss. Perhaps it would be more accurate to say that the break-up of our old social order involves a decline in standards of taste, and the disappearance of that graciousness of living in which they are expressed. Even in the masses there has been a decline. The adolescent boy (or girl), whose literacy is only exercised in the deciphering of comic strips, is less cultured than his illiterate ancestor of a century or two ago, who at the same age had a fund of traditional lore. However difficult it is to make a comparison with the past, and however we explain the facts, it seems certain that our age is relatively deficient in graciousness and poise. This is part of the reason why it has to escape to the dream world of the cinema.

Another point on which it is difficult to compare the present with the past is the extent of crime. Yet, whether we are better or worse than our ancestors, there are criminals in our societies whose conduct infringes the prohibitions which express the minimum requirements of a common life. There always have been criminals, and there are possibly fewer crimes of violence in Europe now than in previous centuries. Men have become unduly complacent, however, about crime, and have failed to see that it is an indication of something wrong with our social life which has not been set right. They have talked much about corrective punishment and the re-education of criminals; but crime is still far from being eliminated.

Finally, it should be noticed that there has been a decline in the influence of all the world religions. Many still profess them, but there is an ever-widening field in which religious considerations are being disregarded. There are differences between the various parts of the world and the various religions, but the general picture is the same. The Christian religion shares in this general decline of religious influence. In addition to this, however, there is a feature which causes serious concern to those who believe that the Christian gospel is the cure for human troubles, namely, the disunity of Christendom. In this disunity the atheist finds some justification for his position. The Christian, on the other hand, maintains that it does not invalidate the claims of the gospel, but that it shows the deep-seated character of the malignant disease from which the world suffers, since even the health-bringing forces are not free from it.

These, then, are some of the more obvious aspects of the troubles of mankind at the present time. The list is incomplete and possibly omits some important matters. Nevertheless, it will be sufficient to introduce the subsequent discussions.

The special features of our age

One question that the preliminary survey raises in our minds is how far the troubles described are due to features of the world situation peculiar to our own time, but absent or insignificant at other times. The mid-twentieth century undoubtedly differs in certain ways from all previous ages, and we must therefore look at its special features to see whether they account for most of our troubles.

The world-shaking change of the last century and a half has been the rapid development of scientific knowledge and of its practical application to man's daily life. The discovery of the principle of the steam engine was followed by the establishment of machine-employing industries and the improvement of communications through railways and steamships. The rate of development in the nineteenth century now seems to us leisurely; yet that century, compared with the previous one, had accomplished a revolution in man's way of living. Moreover, by organizing the activity of research it increased the tempo of discovery. This has resulted in the harnessing of electrical power and the perfecting of wireless communications and broadcasting, while the invention of the internal combustion engine has led to the development of road and air transport. Now we stand on the threshold of the atomic age, with all its potentialities for good and evil. The transformation of human life in the last few decades by the application of scientific discoveries has been so swift that men have hardly begun to grasp its implications. Certain features of this transformation must be given greater prominence to bring out their relevance to the troubles of mankind.

First of all there is the unification of the world. It is now one world in senses in which it has never been one before.

The basic fact is the physical unification. With the appearance of the ordinary telegraph and telephone, and then the wireless telegraph and telephone, the time taken to send a message to any part of the world is negligible. We now take it for granted that all the world should hear of an important event during the twenty-four hours which follow its occurrence; and popular newspapers and broadcasting in general see that our expectations are not disappointed. It is not only news and views, however, that travel rapidly. One V.I.P. now thinks nothing of travelling half round the world and back in order to have a few hours' conversation with another V.I.P. Even the ordinary run of men, if they can lay hands on sufficient money, are able to perform comparable feats by regular passenger flights. Goods, too, where their value justifies it, are transported by air; and apart from this our system of land and sea transportation is such that phenomenally large quantities of goods can be transported over vast distances for a comparatively trifling cost. The extent of our facilities for transportation, when we compare conditions now with those of previous times, is a more important feature of our age than the speed with which we convey selected types of merchandise.

The last point takes us from the physical unification of the world to the economic. Scientific discoveries and their application to industry have led to the growth of mass-production. To set up a factory in which machines take the place of human power is initially expensive; but, once the factory is established, the costs of maintenance and materials are usually small. Consequently, after a certain point the profit per article sold increases greatly, so that, for every additional article sold, not merely does the total profit increase, but the average profit per article increases. Thus, weighty considerations drive manufacturers to extend their markets to the utmost. The steamships and railways of the nineteenth century and the lorries of the twentieth provide the transport. The result of these developments is that the products of European and American factories are used throughout the inhabited world, and that the material basis of civilization is being rapidly unified. The growth of mass-producing industry in Asian and African countries, notably Japan, China, and India, is not reversing the process of unification but rather accelerating it. In these countries factory equipment is usually European, and the industrialists have an eye on European markets; thus the products of the factories are far less in the indigenous tradition than might have been supposed. Behind industry, too, there stands the system of international finance, which in the nineteenth century had entangled eastern countries in its web before they realized its power. Governments are perhaps more fully aware now of the dangers of international finance and take certain precautions; yet the economic interdependence of the world is undoubtedly growing.

The history of the Ottoman Empire in the nineteenth century shows how easy is the passage from economic enterprise to political intervention. The same passage is seen in the history of the Indies, though taking place more slowly. Over three hundred years may be reckoned from the opening of India by Vasco da Gama in 1498—a brilliant application of the new technique of long-distance navigation—to the consolidation of the British Raj in the early nineteenth century. During this period the powers of Western Europe were extending their sway over the less technically developed countries of America, Asia, and Africa, while Russia sprawled over Siberia and Central Asia. In 1914 it looked as if the Europeans were irresistible; but with the growth of political thinking in Asia and Africa, the picture has since been greatly altered.

The attainment of sovereign independence, however, by some Asian and African countries should not be allowed to obscure the fact that political unification is all the time proceeding. History shows that the cohesion of the great empires of antiquity depended on good communications. By 1914 steamships and railways were sufficiently developed to make a world empire a physical possibility; the distance (in time) of the farthest outposts from the capital would have been far less than that of the Roman *limes* from Rome. The Kaiser had doubtless seen this mirage of world empire enticing him to proceed. World empire was also in the thoughts of the leaders of Soviet Russia, but part at least of their plan for attaining it was (and is) the propagating of the Marxist creed. An alternative idea of how the world may be unified is that embodied first in the League of Nations and then in the United Nations Organization. Yet another step towards unification is to be seen in the North Atlantic Treaty Organization. Thus, whatever professions politicians may make, sovereign independence is, in fact, dwindling away and political unification is increasing.

Finally, there is ideological unification. This has followed from the other kinds of unification. For the most part there has been no deliberate propaganda. The rest of the world has been so filled with admiration for European science and technology that it has been eager to acquire these; in the course of doing so it often acquired many other European ideas also, especially secularistic and anti-religious ideas. This latter tendency has not been offset by the successes of Christian missions, since these, impressive as they are, look very small when reduced to percentages. In many areas the most lasting work of Christian missions has been the transmission of European education. In general, however, the European-educated classes neither adopt Christianity, nor retain a vigorous belief in their old religion, but become secularist in outlook. European political ideas, democratic, Marxist, and fascist, have also found their adherents in Asia and Africa, sometimes undergoing a sea-change in the process. In the Islamic world, for example, nationalism has no deep roots—as may be seen from the difficulties of the Arab League; it is largely a stick with which to beat the European who has committed himself to belief in national self-determination. There is a long way to go before ideological unification is complete.

These, then, are the chief ways in which the world has become, and is becoming, one world.

The second feature of the present situation, which is probably something temporary and not permanent, is the disturbance of the social system. This is in large measure the result of the industrial revolution. It is easier for factory hands than for agricultural labourers to discuss their grievances together. As the processes of industry become more complex, too, a higher level of education is required; employees become better able to understand the ways in which they are being exploited, and become open to influences from books and newspapers. Exploitation is almost inevitable in an epoch of sweeping economic changes. The man who has the necessary qualities of mind and character and the necessary opportunities does very well for himself without considering closely the effects of his actions on other people. Even where the employer is benevolent to his employees, there is apt to be jealousy and envy. His former companions, who see him striding ahead of themselves, are envious. The hand-loom weavers who see their livelihood being reduced by the machines have a sense of grievance. In a relatively stable society there is a general recognition that certain inequalities are fair; but when society is changing, as it did in nineteenth-century Britain, all inequalities of wealth or privilege tend to be questioned. The effect of the development of British industry has been the creation of a huge industrial proletariat, which has gradually become better organized and more conscious of its power. It has thus been able to improve its position, chiefly at the expense of sections of the middle classes. The shape of things to come is not yet clear, but there is ample fuel to hand for the fires of class hatred while social climbing is almost universal.

Disturbances of the social system are not confined to Europe. In the Orient, for example, there is an even profounder social upheaval. It is roughly correct to say that, before the impact of Europe, there were two social classes in the Orient, the peasant class (with whom are to be included the handcraftsmen and petty traders subservient to agriculture) and the ruling, land-owning and administrative class. The eagerness for Europeaniza-tion has led to the growth of a new, European-educated middle class, consisting of professional men, civil servants of all grades, other office workers, and skilled artisans. Without these it would be impossible for Oriental countries to function as modern states, but, because they are a new class, they have not yet gained general recognition commensurate with their import-ance. In the Orient, as in Europe, there was much exploitation during the economic changes, but in general it was the more enlightened section of the old upper class that was able to turn the changes to its own account. The first effect of the impact of Europe has thus been to increase inequalities of wealth in the Orient. The old system has broken down; suspicion and distrust have arisen; and, though class feeling is not so bitter as in Europe, it has begun to show itself. All this social unrest is peculiar to the present age.

Finally, there is a certain deterioration in human relationships which looks as if it might be due largely to temporary factors. At least there are temporary factors to which we can point. The establishment of large factories has led to the growth of large towns. Further, most people prefer the amenities, or supposed amenities, of towns to some of the primitive features of country life, and, with improved transport making it possible for men to live a long way from their work, vast urban agglomerations have been formed, of which the London area is the worst. When wage-earners use their homes as dormitories, and when it is easy to move one's house every year or two (as many Londoners seem to prefer), the local community loses all sense of togetherness. A man's next-door neighbours play a negligible part in his life. The individual becomes a mere unit in the mass, unless he is fortunate in belonging to a work-group with a community spirit. Societies and clubs which a man may voluntarily join help to link him up with others. On the whole, however, nothing has yet been devised to take the place of the old village or small-town comunity.

It is curious, however, how the majority of people are more aware of the advantages of towns than of their disadvantages. Perhaps it is because the advantages are material and obvious, like shops and cinemas and schools all near at hand, whereas the disadvantages are *imponderabilia* and by no means obvious. So the movement from the country to the town continues. It is perhaps another effect of the same emphasis on the material and obvious that family life is declining. It is not merely that there are more divorces, and that broadcast appeals daily expose children who have failed to keep in contact with their parents. More than that—even the best of us seem to be losing the art of living together. In pre-European China it was apparently common for as many as five generations to live under one roof; but most of our fellow-countrymen seem to find even part of one generation of "in-laws" intolerable. Is this somehow the result of urbanization, mobility of labour, and similar factors? Certainly there is something wrong.

Machine industry has also altered the attitude of the worker towards his work, which is often monotonous and such that he has no interest in it. He therefore comes to regard the earning of money as the only reason for working. This attitude has also spread even to workers whose work is not uninteresting. Professional men sometimes seem to move to new posts merely in order to obtain a higher salary. So universal is the attitude that we find it difficult to credit the existence of anything else. Yet, in 1942, I visited an old craftsman, a skilled brush-maker, who told me that, on waking up each morning, he thought with pleasure on the work he would be doing during the day. How incredible it seems! The lack of interest and pride in their work which is the experience of most men nowadays has as its complement a false attitude to leisure. People seek excitement in order to make up for the dullness of working hours, or they seek to escape into a dream-world. The cinema provides the easiest form of escape, usually with some sexual excitement thrown in. Popular newspapers whet the jaded appetites with "sensations", often sordid. Young people who have no serious thoughts of marriage, and also older ones, engage in sexual adventures for the sake of excitement, and sexual licence grows. Even before the industrial revolution, of course, men and women were not paragons of respectability in their sexual lives. Yet economic changes (not to mention modern contraceptive devices) seem to have made these problems more serious in our own time.

In general, our relationships with other people have become somewhat impersonal. They are merely other units or items in the mass in which we find ourselves. We care little for them, but we want them to think well of us. If we cannot afford a television set, we at least put up an aerial to make our neighbours believe we are equal to them—as if it mattered what comparative strangers thought of us! Yet it does matter, because in the flux of contemporary society we are all a bit uncertain of ourselves.

Temporary and permanent troubles

The above discussion does not claim to be an exhaustive account of the peculiar troubles of our age, but it is sufficient to show that the special form of the troubles from which we suffer is largely due to special characteristics of our age. That our troubles may be expected to be temporary does not, of course, make them any more tractable for those who have to deal with them. Temporary troubles may prove much more troublesome than permanent ones. Nevertheless it is useful to try to distinguish permanent factors from the temporary ones.

Our most obvious troubles are clearly connected with our

scientific and technological advances. Such are the threat of war, social unrest, and the deterioration of personal relationships. Admiration for scientific achievements has led to over confidence in the possibilities of planning, and to forgetfulness of the areas of human life where planning often fails. At the same time, the religious or intuitional aspect of man's life has become atrophied through this emphasis on the rational aspect. Thus the international, social, and even personal troubles of to-day can be traced to the development of science and technology.

This is not a complete account of the source of the troubles, however. Science and technology lead to economic and other changes. But would these changes lead to troubles such as we are experiencing, unless there was some imperfection in man's response to the situation created by the changes? Why should nations have become more suspicious of one another when they had more frequent contacts? Should not fuller knowledge have led to better understanding? Are there some underlying flaws in human nature that cause men to respond badly to such changes?

It would seem that there are flaws of this sort. The term "selfishness", though vague, might be used to cover them. When in a time of economic change a man does well for himself regardless of other people, he is probably selfish. When members of one class feel bitterly towards members of another, it is perhaps largely selfishness that moves them. Selfishness is not restricted to what concerns the individual's own interests; it may refer to the interests of his family, of his social class, of his country, or of his religious community. There seems to be an element of selfishness in all men. In periods of stability it is held in check by social controls; but with the decline of the social system, it tends to become more prominent.

We speak of periods of stability, as if there had been times when a part of mankind was perfectly adjusted to its environment. In fact, however, mankind has never been perfect. Its adjustment to its environment has never been more than relatively good. Thus no society is ever perfectly equipped to begin responding to changes. Whatever slight imperfections there were in its adjustment to its previous situation might easily be transformed into serious flaws in the course of its efforts to respond to the new situation.

Again, the conservative forces in society, which slow down the response to change, are linked up with selfishness. The conservatism of social tradition is a good thing, and indeed essential to the well-being of society. Social achievements are like a wood; a wood takes years to grow, but a lighted match, thrown away in a careless moment, rapidly destroys everything. Against threats to what grows very slowly, social conservatism is a necessary safeguard. This is a fact which cannot be gainsaid. When we reflect about it, however, we see that it would be more correct to say that there are many situations where social conservatism is good; but when the need is for a new creative response, then to go on conserving is not good. Why do men cling to the past when they should be pioneering? The answer seems to be that this social control is infected with selfishness in the form of fear. Men cling to a few tolerably good things they have and refuse to experiment, because they are afraid that any change may bring something worse.

The last thought suggests that a deeper analysis of selfishness is required, and to this I shall proceed presently. Meanwhile it ought to be clear that our troubles are not due entirely to our environment and to our immediate past. These have created the situations in which the difficulties occurred, but the difficulties have been magnified by imperfections of human nature which, while perhaps not "permanent" in the strict sense, are of more than temporary character.

2 THE ROOT OF OUR TROUBLES

It is commonly admitted that mankind is imperfect. Many people, of course, would be inclined to say that there is a section of mankind (to which they themselves belong) which is only slightly imperfect; they might even think that the imperfections of this section are negligible. Yet nearly everyone, when pressed, admits that mankind as a whole is imperfect, and even that he himself is imperfect. In view of this it is curious that so little effort has been expended in the present century on attempting to analyse further this universal imperfection of mankind. Is it because the researcher would have to admit his partial incompetence, seeing that he is involved in the imperfection he is studying?

Incomplete diagnoses

While there is a scarcity of explicit diagnoses of man's imperfections, there is a plethora of cures offered for the symptoms from which he suffers, and these generally imply some diagnosis. I shall consider two lines of thought on the matter, partly because they are interesting in themselves, but even more because discussion of them will bring to light points that will be useful in the subsequent investigations.

The first line of thought is what may be called "the popular religious view". It appears to be widespread in this country, though it is probably not often clearly expressed, since it would hardly satisfy responsible religious leaders. It is derived from Christian thought, but it is something of a caricature of that, and I mention it here in order to distinguish it from the more orthodox Christian views to be expressed later. This popular religious view, then, is somewhat as follows: "On the whole men know what is right. Where there is ignorance of right and wrong, it can easily be remedied. Our troubles arise from the fact that men do not do what they know to be right. This may come about through negligence or through weakness of will. In either case men can obtain through religion power to enable them to overcome their faults, so that they nearly always do what they know to be right."

This line of thought as here expressed is open to the objection that it is irreligious, since it attempts to use Divine power in order to achieve human ends. The view could, of course, be reformulated to avoid this error, but it would seem that it is in fact the irreligious form of the view that predominates in this country. The view is not confined to this country or to Christianity. There are young Muslim intellectuals who maintain that the principles of Islam would lead to a peaceful world community, if only men accepted them and practised them. We need not therefore look any farther at the religious aspects of the view, but may turn to the implied diagnosis of the imperfection of human nature.

According to this diagnosis, the source of human troubles is lack of moral effort, amounting in some cases to weakness of will. Men do not make a serious attempt to do what they know to be right, nor, where they are uncertain, to find out what is right. Much of this is merely slackness or complacency. Sometimes they are carried away by passion, or unable to resist their desires; and then we speak of weakness of will. Both slackness and weakness of will, it is commonly held, can be eliminated by religion or—perhaps a growing number of people would say— by psychological methods.

This account of the root of human troubles is open to several objections. For one thing it smacks of old *laisser-faire* doctrines, especially of the idea that, where individuals are good and upright in their personal relationships, the economic, social, and political order of their society is bound to be satisfactory. The Europe of to-day, however, has seen the abuses which appeared in a society dominated by *laisser-faire*, and it wants to have no more of them. Apart from this connection with *laisser-faire*, the inadequacy of this diagnosis of human troubles is seen in its failure to explain conflicts where both sides have many good and upright people and both sides believe they are right—for instance, in some of the cases of conflict or disunity between Christian bodies. In such cases there is no agreement about what is right and good, and the absence of agreement is not due to the vicious and perverted outlook of one side—at least in the opinion of most impartial observers. Both sides have beliefs about values, beliefs which they hold conscientiously, but these beliefs clash. Many of the most stubborn political disputes are also of this type. Such difficulties cannot be met simply by greater self-control and more sustained efforts to realize one's moral ideal.

Recent decades, too, have made mankind aware that it is not merely the instinctive desires that divert a man from doing what is right. Irrational forces of great power have swept over whole societies of men and plunged them into evil. The phenomena are best described as instances of communal neurosis. In a notoriously bad case the society becomes a danger to other societies. A dispassionate reading of history, however, leads to the conclusion that no society is completely free from at least the possibility of neurosis. Beneath the conscious life of societies there slumber autonomous complexes which in certain conditions might wake up and become active. Before we realize it, our own society may begin to move under the sway of such an irrational force, and all the subtleties of reason and the determination of the moral will would be powerless to halt it. To describe such an experience as "weakness of will" is to use too mild a term. It is more like "demonic possession", but science is still too close to its materialistic phase for this term to be given a scientific meaning. Without further consideration, therefore, of the nature of these irrational forces which "carry away" men and societies, let us acknowledge the inadequacy of the diagnosis of human imperfection implicit in the "popular religious view".

The second line of thought on this matter which I want to mention is that connected with the word "planning". Planning, of course, is so much one of the master concepts of our time that almost every intellectual group is under its influence to some extent. The anti-rational pietist is no more exempt than the anti-rational political extremist. All are organizing their movements and planning for advance. All are speaking about their problems and how to solve them—which implies that the difficulties they encounter are "problems" that can be surmounted by the application of human intelligence.

This application of human intelligence in our responses to the environment is the essence of planning. Planning is thus a normal part of all human life. Indeed, a life could hardly be said to be human if there were no planning in it. There are areas where spontaneity is desirable, and where planning is therefore injurious in so far as it checks spontaneity. Apart from these areas, however, it would seem that the ideal is to plan as fully and carefully as possible. To this extent I am a whole-hearted believer in planning. What I want to criticize is not planning as such, but the belief that the fundamental human troubles are such that they can be eliminated by planning. This belief may take many forms. If the root of our troubles is regarded as ignorance, then planning will be primarily education. If, on the other hand, our troubles are thought of as due to the action of natural forces which are indifferent to human welfare, then the planning will be mainly scientific and technological, and will probably have to be under political control. The recalcitrance of human beings to the chances involved in large-scale long-distance planning can be largely overcome, partly by school education and partly by control of broadcasting and the press; news and views are now disseminated chiefly by broadcasting and by a few popular newspapers with a large circulation, and it is therefore easy for totalitarian governments to mould public opinion.

This is not the place to consider the merits and demerits of political planning and to discuss its proper limits. Our concern at the moment is whether the root trouble of mankind is such that it can be cured by planning, and various considerations combine to make it almost certain that it is not.

One point is that, even where several groups of people are in general agreement about some end, it is often impossible for planners to draw up a detailed plan which all the groups will be prepared to accept. This is constantly happening in politics. Different countries may agree about a general end, but be unable to agree about the means of realizing this end in practice. Even where there is a large measure of good-will on all sides, it may be infinitely difficult to have a detailed plan accepted. Many Christian bodies now want Christian unity, but have made little progress towards the practical achievement of unity. Men have a security within a smaller community which they are afraid may be lacking within a larger community. They have their beliefs about what is important and their appreciation of values, and these are deep-seated things which are not readily changed. This whole area of feelings and valuations is in general beyond the reach of the rational procedures which are the stock-in-trade of the planner—even in many cases beyond the psychological methods open to a totalitarian dictator.

On the other hand, this region of feelings and valuations, though beyond the reach of planning, is open to the working of irrational forces. The phenomena of religious conversion in individuals are familiar to psychologists. A religious conversion that is mild and unspectacular from the observer's standpoint may produce a complete transformation of the man's valuations and revolutionary changes in his feelings. In religious conversions the transformations and changes are usually for the better, but when irrational forces sweep over a nation the changes may be for the worse. Against such movements of the spirit, whether good or bad, planning is powerless. A clear-sighted planner may sometimes notice the swell of the ocean before it is generally observed, and may manage for a time to ride in on the crest of the wave; but that is the most that is possible. The movements of the spirit in nations and in individuals flood and ebb with as little regard for planners as the tide had for King Canute.

The diagnosis of human imperfection implicit in the view that planning is the panacea for all human ills is thus inadequate. Planning must always be planning for an end, and it therefore only works where the society for whom the planning is done agrees—or is made to agree—about the end. But the acceptance of ends, both of supreme ends and also, in some cases, of subordinate ends, is something that cannot be planned. Our investigation of this line of thought about the cure for human troubles, like that of the previous line of thought, has yielded only negative results. It will be worth while, however, before proceeding to go over some of the phenomena of human imperfection that have been mentioned in passing. These are symptoms that must not be lost sight of in diagnosis.

One symptom is the difference in men's valuations and the difficulty in inducing them to change these. Men differ in the comparative importance they assign to different things, and in respect of what things are to be accepted as ends, supreme or subordinate. Sometimes we may dismiss these valuations as prejudice; sometimes we may allow that they are conscientiously held opinions. In either case they are deep-seated and a man is seldom ready to abandon them. Now some differences in valuations in the members of a society are compatible with harmonious life in the society as a whole. Thus some men may prefer town to country, some country to town, and some may be indifferent; and if the proportions are about correct (with regard to the needs of the society) and those with preferences are able to have what they prefer, then the society should be happy, at least in this respect. Unfortunately, not all differences in valuation are of this kind. One man's set of values may bring him into conflict with other members of his society. Even when members of a society acknowledge the same values (for example when they all consider material luxuries to be of great import-ance), they may be in conflict with one another because of these values. Finally, a system of values which leads to a harmonious life within the society, may bring the society into conflict with other societies with which it is in contact.

Differences of the latter kind, that is, those producing dis-harmony, are an indication that the system of values is not sound. When the system of values in a society is sound, the life of that society over a period of generations will be harmonious and meaningful. The problem before mankind in our age may be said to be to find a sound system of values for the whole of mankind, and to secure universal acceptance of this system. On the other hand, our systems of values are all to some extent un-sound. In so far as this is so, it means that certain aspects of the nature of our societies do not have an adequate part in the conscious life of the societies. Consequently there is a likelihood, amounting almost to certainty, that compensatory movements will appear in the unconscious of the society, that is, in the unconscious of members of the society. If these compensatory movements are integrated into the conscious life of the society, that life will be enriched and new possibilities of harmony will be opened up. If the compensatory movements are not integrated, however, they will lead to neurosis and psychosis, and at the worst we may have the mass-psychosis of a whole society.

Further, it must be insisted that the symptoms described in the last two paragraphs are universal. Some individuals and societies have sets of values that are much less sound than those of others; some are much farther than others from an integrated life. All, however, suffer to some extent from unsound values, and from neurosis or psychosis. "All", too, here includes not only the people alive to-day, but also all past generations and all those to be born in the foreseeable future. The imperfections found in men in respect of their valuations and their degree of integration are passed on to their descendants by heredity and environment. Movements of integration appear from time to time, and in certain centuries mankind may be seen to be moving slowly upward. There have also been catastrophic intervals, however, when the forces of disintegration appeared to be stronger than the forces of integration, and when much of the ground gained was lost.

These, then, are some of the symptoms that must be accounted for in any general view of the essential nature of human imperfection.

Towards a fuller diagnosis

I now come to the most speculative assertion in this book. It would have been possible to proceed without giving more than a general account of the root of human troubles. It seems more advantageous, however, to put forward a definite hypothesis, since in this way the whole discussion will gain in concreteness. Should it be found—as is probable—that the hypothesis is in need of revision, its very definiteness will be an aid in the work of reformulation.

I assert, then, by way of hypothesis, that those human imperfections which underlie the troubles of mankind are primarily due to the appearance of self-consciousness in man. This assertion, of course, requires some elucidation and explanation.

By "self-consciousness" is meant awareness of oneself as a continuing or enduring entity. In thus becoming aware of himself a man forms a picture of himself, but his picture is usually an inadequate one, not merely in the sense of being incomplete (which would not necessarily have any bad consequences), but in the sense of falsifying important details. Most of us, for example, think more highly than we are justified in doing of our talents and achievements. In terms of Jungian psychology, what most men have is an ego-consciousness, not a consciousness of the "self", that is, of their being as a whole. From some points of view this might look like a difference of degree, though Jung speaks of it as a difference in kind. In general it may be said that the self-consciousness of different human beings differs in various ways. Self-consciousness does not appear to exist in animals, though the evidence is difficult to interpret; if self-consciousness is found in animals, it can only be in a rudimentary form.

To trace human troubles to the appearance of self-consciousness does not imply that before man became aware of himself he was perfect. Before man appeared on the earth, animals had preyed on other animals, and there had been all the pain from hunger, wounds, disease, and the action of parasites. If we suppose that man lived for some time on the earth before he attained self-consciousness, man also must have suffered in these ways. What is the meaning, then, of saying that human troubles are due to the appearance of self-consciousness? Prior to its appearance we must suppose man to have had an awareness of the world which in some respects was wider than ours, but at the same time was less differentiated or articulated. The individual must have been aware of himself as a member of his community, but this awareness would be unanalysed; it would not occur to him to think of himself as distinct from the community. When he felt pain, he would respond to the feeling by trying to stop it or avoid it. Through memory he would have some ideas about cause and effect, and he would thus to some extent be able to anticipate future occurrences of the pain and to avoid them. If we may put his experience into words, it would be "this is bad", and that would imply that something had to be done about it; but his experience would not be "this is bad for me", since he would have no conception of "me" with which to connect the pain.

In attaining to self-consciousness such an individual becomes aware of himself in his separation and distinction from his fellows. That is to say, his attention is directed to one aspect of his relationship to his fellows—his differentiation from them —and he neglects the complementary aspect of their close association with one another in the community. Previously he was dimly aware of both aspects together, though neither was explicit. Now in becoming explicitly aware of his separation, he has become largely unconscious of his association with others and that they all belong together. When he suffers from a pain from which others apparently do not suffer, it tends to make him more fully aware of his isolation and weakness and insecurity. Then, to compensate for this there occurs inflation of the ego. He tries to make himself feel more secure by emphasizing his powers and his virtues. With pride he remembers his past achievements. In his picture of himself his good qualities (those of which he approves) are exaggerated, and his bad qualities softened down or even omitted altogether. Thus at best the individual with his self-consciousness has become selfish, at worst he has become neurotic.

The appearance of an ego-consciousness in the individual member of a group is the most obvious way for self-consciousness to appear, but it is not the only way. Historically there is usually a prior stage, namely, the appearance of a group-consciousness. This means that members of a group come to be aware of the separation and distinction of their group from other groups. The appearance of self-consciousness in this communal form has similar effects to its appearance in an individual form. The previous dim awareness of their group as both distinct from other groups, and also as belonging together with them, is lost. As men become more explicitly aware of the first aspect, they cease to be conscious at all of the second aspect. They are intensely aware of the isolation of their group. It is alone in a hostile world; they are afraid that it may be destroyed by enemies or may not have enough food. By way of compensation they exaggerate the virtues and achievements of the group, and group-pride develops. Pre-Islamic Arabic poetry is a good example of group-consciousness. The poems are in the main tribal, for individualism was only beginning to appear among the nomads, and fall into two classes: those in which the poet recalls the glories of his own tribe, and those in which he pours contempt on the weaknesses and disgraces of hostile tribes.

Thus in two ways the appearance of self-consciousness is at the root of human troubles. It is not merely that the appearance of the individual's ego-consciousness warps his view of the world and of his place in it, especially his place in his group or society. Prior to this, the appearance of what we may call a we-consciousness in the members of the society has warped their view of their society's place in the world. This may be put in another way by referring to values. A man's valuations are largely determined for him by his society. If the society's outlook is not perfectly balanced, its system of values will be imperfect. Thereafter the individual, with his imperfectly balanced outlook, has to adapt the already imperfect system of values to his special position in his society and his other special circumstances. Thus there is a double possibility of corruption in human valuations. In the world as we know it, too, the valuations and moral system of a society have been adjusted to the imperfect character of the members of the society. A large measure of selfishness is assumed. Society induces its members to perform socially useful functions by offering material rewards such as money, or immaterial rewards such as titles and other public honours.

There appears to be a close connection between valuations and self-consciousness. Prior to self-consciousness man undoubtedly has his preferences; that is, he will normally prefer a thing of one kind to a thing of another kind. This order of preference, however, is not a conscious principle. That is to say, a particular man may always prefer apples to pears, if he has a choice, but he does not formulate to himself the principle that "apples are better than pears". It is conceivable, of course, that such a principle could be formulated independently of self-consciousness. For it to be a *principle*, however, that is, a rule which man follows in all circumstances, implies that the man is aware of himself as an enduring entity which acts in many different situations. Thus explicit beliefs in values presuppose self-consciousness. At the same time self-consciousness is largely constituted by the valuations current in the man's society. An important part of a man's picture of himself is the *persona*, that is, the socially-determined conception of the acts and qualities proper to a man performing his function in the society.

The tendency to neurosis is also closely connected with self-consciousness. Before the appearance of self-consciousness there were doubtless occasions when a man's activity showed a lack of integration. His hunger or anger might overcome his prudence and lead him to do something which he realized was foolish. This might be interpreted, however, as a failure of the principle of integration in the man to control a part of him, namely, his hunger. The appearance of an ego-consciousness, however, and the resultant tendency for autonomous complexes to grow and develop in the unconscious, seems to indicate corruption in the very centre of the man, in his principle of integration. The principle of integration in the man is not identical with his ego-consciousness. It is rather the Jungian "self" of which the man only becomes aware on the completion of the process of individuation. In certain contexts it may be convenient to speak of the autonomous complex as a part of the man which has split off. It is part of the "self", however; it is not something which is properly subordinate to the principle of integration, but a manifestation of that principle. With the heightening of a man's awareness of one aspect of the integrative activities that go on in his being (that is, in the formation of an ego-consciousness), he tends to lose what awareness he had of other aspects, and it becomes possible for these to generate autonomous complexes in the unconscious. Thus neurosis presupposes the appearance of self-consciousness.

There seems to be a strong case, then, for the hypothesis that has been put forward, namely, that the troubles of mankind arise chiefly from imperfections in man which are due to the appearance of self-consciousness. This apparently harmless change leads man to adopt inadequate and injurious systems of value-judgements and makes him liable to neurosis. In such circumstances it is not surprising that reason or consciousness is unable to bring about in the world that peace which most men consciously desire, and that whole societies are swept off their feet by irrational movements.

3 THE TRADITIONAL CHRISTIAN ACCOUNT

The account of human troubles so far given has been at the secular level. Since I am engaged in expounding the Christian gospel, however, I must attempt to show that this secular analysis of our troubles is at least roughly equivalent to the Christian diagnosis. Unfortunately, this Christian diagnosis is not so clear as one would have liked. The popular Christian view which has already been mentioned is a simplification of New Testament teaching, but it is inadequate to explain the facts, and in some respects is misleading as a guide to the New Testament. Responsible Christian theologians have recognized the shortcomings of the popular view, but there seems to be no clear and generally accepted alternative.

The nature of sin

The traditional Christian account of human troubles is that they are due to man's sin. On this there would be general agreement. The difficulties begin when an attempt is made to describe sin. If sins are taken to be acts contrary to the will of God, then a distinction has to be drawn between material and formal sins, that is, between acts which are contrary to the will of God, whether the agent knows it or not, and acts which the agent believes to be contrary to the will of God, whether they are in fact contrary or not. In terms of this distinction, only those acts are sins which are both materially and formally sinful. Attention is thus directed to those acts which are in fact contrary to the will of and which the agent, believing them to be contrary to the will of God, consciously and voluntarily performs. Theological discussions of sin recognize that there are other kinds of sin, but they tend to concentrate on those aspects of the subject related to man's responsibility and guilt. For the Christian minister dealing with men and women in spiritual difficulties these aspects are of great importance. Nevertheless, as it stands, the popular view of sin is inadequate to account for all the troubles of the world.

The New Testament gives a much more comprehensive account of the origin of human troubles. Saint Paul speaks of the "wiles of the devil" and reminds Christians that their wrestling is "not against flesh and blood, but against principalities, against powers, against the rulers of the darkness of this world, against spiritual wickedness in high places" (Eph. 6. 11 f.). Whatever precisely was intended by these phrases, it presumably included the irrational forces which are liable to dominate man's unconscious. The phrase "the world, the flesh and the devil", which will presently be discussed, may be regarded as a rough equivalent.

If, then, we take the traditional Christian account of the source of human troubles to be more comprehensive than the popular view of sin, can it be maintained that it is essentially the same as the secular account given in the previous sections?

In accordance with the views maintained in *The Reality of God*, I regard the universe as a whole within which are to be distinguished subordinate wholes arranged hierarchically. Thus the totality of mankind forms a whole to which are subordinated the various national and other societies of men. These societies are themselves wholes, whose parts are individual human beings; and each human being is also a whole and within him are lesser wholes. Each whole has a principle of integration which is in part immanent and in part transcendent. The principle of integration of the universe is God.

Now sin is human activity contrary to the will of God. The will of God, however, can be understood in two ways, which may be distinguished as the general will of God and his particular will. The general will of God is what would happen in the universe if the whole of it at some previous time had been brought into subordination to him as supreme principle of integration, and if it was now functioning in due subordination to him. The particular will of God, on the other hand, is what would happen if the whole universe in its present imperfect condition suddenly began to function in due subordination to God. The general will of God is thus the ideal of what the universe would be if all its imperfections were removed. The particular will of God is the ideal of the best attainable in a concrete situation where there are many imperfections. This distinction is due to the fact that many human imperfections are such that they cannot quickly be remedied, but only after years or generations. Even if all men were suddenly to resolve to do the will of God in the particular situations in which they found themselves, and were all to remain faithful to this resolve, there would still be many imperfections both in the individual men and in their society. This implies that many human imperfections are not *necessarily* contrary to the particular will of God, though actually most of them probably are contrary to it. What may be asserted, however, of the human imperfections, which in the previous sections were asserted to be at the root of our troubles, is that they are contrary to the general will of God. In this sense, therefore, they are sins.

This conclusion may appear to be harmless, but the appearance is misleading. Among the imperfections described, a prominent place was given to false valuations and tendencies to neurosis. Consequently the conclusion means that human activity based on false valuations is sinful, and that activity of a neurotic character is sinful. This is opposed to what men commonly believe, for most of us have been infected with the idea that the question of sin is mainly, or entirely, a question of individual guilt, and in the kinds of activity mentioned it is commonly thought that there is no guilt, or only a slight degree of guilt. If anyone cares to argue that sin properly connotes guilt, I shall not oppose his use of the word, but only assert that sin in this restricted sense is not adequate as an account of the source of our troubles, and is probably not what is meant in the New Testament. Our troubles, I firmly believe, or rather the imperfect activities which lead to them, are contrary to the will of God. If one defines sin as human activity contrary to the will of God, then the conclusion seems inevitable that these activities are sinful.

It may be objected that a human activity, to be sinful, must be conscious and voluntary, and that activity based on false valuations and neurotic activity is not fully conscious and voluntary. In reply to this objection it might be pointed out that the question of guilt is here coming into the foreground. A man is only justly to be blamed and punished for a bad act if he was fully conscious of what he was doing, and did it voluntarily and deliberately. This question, I must insist, is of limited interest and often of secondary importance. Consider the share of Hitler in bringing about the second World War. Was he acting consciously and voluntarily, or was he suffering from a mental disease which made him not responsible for his actions? Compared with the fact that war occurred and that Hitler's activity contributed to its outbreak, the question of his degree of guilt is academic. If we suppose a similar occasion in the future when a dictator gains the power to plunge the world into war, the concern of the rest of mankind would be stop him, whether he is responsible for his actions or not; they would not be concerned with discovering what, if he did cause a war, was the precise degree of his guilt. A knowledge of his state of mind would be important only in so far as it might help them to stop him.

Moreover, an act may be a truly human act and may be properly attributed to a man even where it was not fully conscious and voluntary. It is actually very difficult to say when an act is voluntary and fully conscious. Mostly men are satisfied with a relatively high degree of these qualities, and indeed an absolute degree seems to be impossible. To be fully conscious of what one was doing in any particular act one would really need to be omniscient. On the other hand, a man whose activity has been neurotic, or based on false valuations, may come to a sounder frame of mind in which he is aware of the imperfections in his activity, and may be willing to acknowledge the activity as his, and say "I did that". Again, because a man acted in ignorance, whether of facts or of values, what he did does not cease to be his act. Because of his ignorance the guilt attaching to him is less, but his ignorance does not reduce the damage and loss caused by the act. When one is considering the troubles of mankind and the possibility of applying a remedy, this second point of view is of primary importance, while the question of individual guilt is largely irrelevant. Since this book is dealing with human troubles and their cure, sin will be understood in the widest sense as including all human activity contrary to the will of God.

The connection between sin as thus conceived and the human imperfections described in the foregoing secular analysis may be illustrated by the traditional view that sin is linked with the world, the flesh, and the devil. The flesh is the easiest of these to understand. It may be roughly translated by "instincts"; but it must be remembered that these instincts occur in human beings who are imperfect because of the one-sided development of their ego-consciousness. This means that sins of the flesh are normally not a mere yielding to instinctive drives, but that other factors are involved. By the "world" as a source of sin is meant the corrupt and imperfect condition of the society in which an individual finds himself. Since the valuations of the individual are largely determined by those current in his society, false valuations in his society will lead him to perform acts contrary to the will of God. In particular, imperfections in the society will be reflected in his *persona*. It is more difficult to say what is meant by the "devil". Perhaps the devil is a projection of internal tendencies to neurosis; but this suggestion can hardly be discussed at the moment, since the idea of projection requires a deeper investigation than can be given to it here. What we may say is that in neuroses we have evidence of an integrative activity in the individual, distinct from his principle of integration, and that this integrative activity is directed towards his destruction and sometimes also that of his society. Whether this integrative activity also transcends the individual, or whether its apparent transcendence is the result of projection, must be left undecided.

From this discussion of the nature of sin the important point which emerges is that, when we are concerned to find a remedy for human troubles, we must direct our attention, not to the sins which men consciously and deliberately commit (serious as these are), but to the sins which they commit without being aware that their activity is contrary to the will of God.

The fall and original sin

In the traditional Christian accounts the actual sins of men are asserted to be derived in some sense from the sin of Adam in eating the fruit of the tree of the knowledge of good and evil. This doctrine of the fall of man, as it is called, is thus an attempt to explain the universal occurrence of sin in the human race. The doctrine is therefore parallel to the hypothetical assertion made above that the appearance of self-consciousness is the source of the fundamental human imperfections. Can this assertion be squared with the story of the fall of man as it occurs in the book of Genesis and with the use made of the story by Saint Paul and others? Many points are made in the course of the story, and all could be included in our treatment in one fashion or another; but it will suffice to concentrate on one or two points.

It is usually said that, while all men are subject to original sin, it appears in them not as any actual sin imputable to them but as a tendency to sin. This fits in very well with our hypothesis about self-consciousness, if by "actual sin" here is meant an act for which a man may properly be blamed or held responsible (and this seems to be the sense required by the context). The possession of an imperfect ego-consciousness is not an actual sin in this sense, but it easily leads to activities and attitudes that are sinful. To have an awareness of oneself as an enduring entity is indeed a step forward, if the awareness is sound. In the same way the knowledge of good and evil conferred by the fruit of the forbidden tree must have been a step forward. This makes it puzzling that God should have forbidden Adam and Eve to eat the fruit of the tree. The puzzle disappears, however, if we suppose that the prohibition was intended to be temporary. The sin of Adam would then consist in trying to obtain the knowledge of good and evil—or in snatching at self-consciousness—before the proper time. This would imply, in modern secular terms, that man, had he not snatched prematurely, could have passed smoothly to a sound self-consciousness instead of to an imperfect ego-consciousness. This is mainly an academic question, and the evidence on which to base a reply to it is scanty. Men as we know them usually find it easier to study the separate trees than to see the wood as a whole. There seems to be no cogent reason, however, for denying the possibility that men, had they not gone astray, might in time have passed to a sound self-consciousness.

The effects of original sin were transmitted from Adam to

his descendants. This transmission is commonly held to be by heredity, but there is nothing in the book of Genesis or in the earliest Christian theology to prevent the transmission being in part through environmental influences. Similarly, once self-consciousness had appeared in man, it passed to later generations. It probably first appeared in man, and not in the lower animals, and it was probably a we-consciousness to begin with rather than an ego-consciousness. It is impossible to say whether self-consciousness appeared spontaneously only in one group or individual, and spread from this point to the rest of mankind, or whether it appeared independently at a number of points. In either case environment was probably mainly responsible for the spread of self-consciousness, though heredity doubtless also contributed by transmitting a tendency to develop in this way. In these respects, then, there is a rough—though not an exact—equivalence between original sin in the traditional account and the appearance of self-consciousness.

It is further stated traditionally that it is because of original sin that human beings are subject to death, that women suffer great pain in child-birth, and that men wrest a living from the fields only by wearisome effort. Now it cannot be held that death in itself is due to the growth of an ego-consciousness; but there are some grounds for maintaining that imperfect self-consciousness is the reason for the bitterness of man's experience of death. That experience includes the gloom of the prospect of death, the suffering often involved in dying, and the bereavement of the survivors. The bitterness of such experiences is increased when a man ceases to be fully aware of how he and the rest of the universe belong together, and when in weakness of body and spirit he is unable to escape from the thought of his isolation. Without self-consciousness men would be dimly aware of their togetherness with the universe and would not have the feeling of loneliness and isolation. After a death the survivors would not think of what *they* had lost but—in much the same way as an infant who has lost father or mother—would devote themselves to the tasks confronting them. Thus most of the bitterness of death would seem to come from our imperfect ego-consciousness. It is a matter of observation that devout Christians, who have presumably attained freedom from many of the imperfections of the ego-consciousness, frequently have easy deaths, whereas less religious persons have a long and difficult struggle.

The other effects of original sin in the traditional account, namely, the pains of travail and the weary toil of agriculture, are of less theological importance; but in these also self-consciousness may be seen to have an influence. There is a body of medical opinion which holds that much of the pain of births is due to anxiety, for anxiety leads to a contraction of the muscles which increases the difficulty of labour. Certainly in large sections of society—chiefly among women, of course—there is a fear of the pain, difficulty, and danger of child-birth that is out of all proportion to the medical facts. This fear, too, propagates itself; as they wait in pre-natal clinics women tell one another blood-curdling stories. So confidence is undermined and fear increases. When a woman's time comes, her muscles are taut, and her labour much worse than it need have been. This cannot all be blamed directly on self-consciousness; but much of it arises from the feeling of insecurity in society which is largely due to self-consciousness.

The toil of agricultural labour may be taken to stand for the wearisome and irksomeness of all work. In the world as it is constituted man must presumably work in order to keep himself alive, quite apart from the presence or absence of self-consciousness. Man's feeling, however, that his work is wearisome and irksome is another matter; and it would be plausible to regard this feeling as due chiefly to self-consciousness. In so far as man thinks of himself as separate from the rest of the universe, and does not understand the place of pain and suffering in the scheme of things, he finds in work something which prevents him living his life as he wants to live it, and as he thinks he has a right to live it. Work is imposed upon him by the threat of starvation, if he is a peasant, or by the threat of socially unpleasant consequences, if he is a factory worker in a welfare state. An imperfect ego-consciousness makes a man see in his work an unfair imposition and a heavy burden, and to this extent is the source of an unsound attitude towards work.

Finally, let us look at the connection between self-consciousness and the seven capital or basic sins, which are the source of all actual sins, namely, pride, envy, anger, covetousness, gluttony, lust, and sloth. Pride is usually reckoned the worst of the seven, and in some ways the most fundamental. This accords with our hypothesis about self-consciousness, for in psychological terms pride is the inflation of the ego, and this inflation tends to occur by way of compensation when a man thinks of himself as distinct from his group and from the rest of mankind. Envy is essentially the feeling of inferiority at the sight of other men's goods. To it there contribute the sense of one's own separateness and the absence of a sense of partnership with the other man. Anger—that is, the emotion, not the instinct—may be regarded as a compensation for weakness. Covetousness is the desire to amass things not strictly necessary, and luxuries. It is connected with the false valuations derived from the "world", and it serves to counteract the feeling of insecurity of the isolated ego. Gluttony, sexual lust, and sloth, from which spring the sins of the flesh, are probably not so purely animal as they appear to be. In many cases it would seem that a man turns to "fleshly" indulgence as a compensation for a feeling of weakness or inferiority. Thus all the seven basic sins are intimately connected with self-consciousness, and it might not be too much to say that the activities corresponding to them would not be sinful if there were no self-consciousness. Since all actual sins spring from one or more of these basic sins, there is a sense in which all actual sins are due to an imperfect self-consciousness.

In conclusion, then, it may be asserted that the effects of the appearance of self-consciousness in man are roughly the same as those of original sin, and that therefore the secular analysis of human troubles in the earlier part of this chapter, despite the differences of terminology, is essentially identical with the traditional Christian diagnosis.

2

THE ESSENTIAL CURE

THE CHRISTIAN claims that in Jesus what was wrong with the world has been set right, and in the present chapter, against the background of the preceding analysis of human troubles, an attempt will be made to elucidate this claim by reformulating the achievement of Jesus in modern terms. It should be noted that the claim is not that all that is wrong with the world has in fact already been put right, but that for the tendencies leading to wrong there have been substituted tendencies leading to right. To vary the metaphor, the claim is not that all human troubles have been cured in detail, but that they have been cured in essence or in principle, and that the healing medicines are now available for those who care to apply them. Leaving the application of the cure to be dealt with in the following chapter, then, I now turn to the consideration of the essential cure.

I THE CURATIVE ACTION OF GOD IN THE OLD TESTAMENT

In order to understand the achievement of Jesus we must look at the situation confronting him. The primary material for this is to be found in the New Testament, but we require to supplement this by some knowledge of the history of the Jews in the previous centuries and, more particularly, by an appreciation of the Old Testament history which played a large part in forming the outlook of the contemporaries of Jesus. In speaking of the curative action of God as conceived and recorded in the Old Testament, I do not intend to suggest that this was the only remedial movement before Jesus. All religions may be said to be attempting to cure human troubles, at least on a local scale; and, though some attempted cures may have made the disease worse, on the whole the great world-religions have been an influence for good. The reason for putting special emphasis on the religion described in the Old Testament is not the value it has in itself, great as that is, but its historical connection with Jesus.

At the centre of the Old Testament is Israel's belief in God, that is, their conviction that there was a great power in the universe supporting them. At first their conception of God was imperfect. They thought there were other beings similar to him, and specially connected with other tribes just as he was specially connected with them; but these other beings were weaker than God. Gradually they came to realize that God, the great power whom they worshipped, was the supreme power in the universe. Moreover, despite his greatness, he was specially attentive to their welfare, and they stood in a special relation to him. This special relationship was described by the picture of a "covenant" or "testament" between God and Israel (from which the name of the "Old Testament" is derived), and it was held that in this the initiative was God's and that he had chosen Israel.

These ideas are clearly relevant to the troubles caused by the appearance of self-consciousness, especially in the form of group-consciousness. The group that is aware of itself as a group distinct from other groups, tends to feel weak and isolated. Belief in God led Israel to see that it was supported by the strength of the supreme power in the universe, and its special relation to this power meant that it was no longer isolated. The mere enunciation of such ideas, of course, would not have been very helpful. Ideas require to be assisted to gain acceptance, in order that they may lead to deep conviction. For Israel the ideas were vigorously confirmed by a theistic interpretation of history. The escape of Israel from Egypt, its settlement in Palestine, its restoration from exile and many lesser events, were regarded as acts of God; even the exile itself was an act of God punishing his chosen people. From the spiritual leaders, who first understood this significance of the historical events, the conviction spread to the people as a whole that the supreme power in the universe had delivered them from their enemies and was working for them. This is the primary aspect of the curative process.

For most of the Old Testament period the problems raised by the self-consciousness of the group were more pressing than those raised by the self-consciousness of the individual. The latter appear chiefly in the form of selfishness in conduct. There is for the most part little concern for the fate of the individual after death. Even in New Testament times, belief in the immortality of the individual was not universal among the Jews; the gospels and the *Acts* show us that, though the Pharisees maintained the belief, the rival party, the Sadducees, opposed it. In the Old Testament, therefore, the chief way in which an imperfect ego-consciousness is corrected is by the realization that God makes demands in respect of conduct and worship on those whom he specially supports. The conduct demanded is the minimum needed for a reasonably harmonious functioning of the society. The function of the worship demanded is to knit the society together in common acts and to increase its confidence as it faces its environment, human and non-human. In these ways the convictions of Israel lead towards a fuller integration of the society.

It was originally thought that the continuance of God's favour to Israel depended on Israel's fulfilment of God's demands. In course of time, however, it was realized that Israel sometimes fell far short of fulfilling the demands, that is, sinned against God, but that despite this, God, provided Israel repented, would forgive the past sins and would continue his favour to Israel. The appreciation of this continuing love of God for a sinful people, and his readiness to forgive, was the achievement of the great prophets whose books are contained in the Old Testament. The prophets' call to national repentance was an important corrective of the inflated group-consciousness, or, more simply, pride, which had resulted from the awareness of their special relationship to the supreme power in the universe. There had been a widespread tendency to think of the expected "day of the Lord" as a time when God would give them the victory over all their neighbours, whether they had fulfilled his demands or not. This false conception of Israel's place in the universe and its relation to God was partly corrected by the prophets' hints that the "day of the Lord" might be not a day of victory for Israel, but a day of punishment for their shortcomings.

The danger remained, however, of an inflation of the group-consciousness of Israel. It was gradually realized that the demands of God applied not merely to Israel, but also in some measure to all the other communities in the world. This led to a fuller appreciation of the greatness of God and the comparative littleness of Israel; "the Lord sitteth upon the circle of the world, and the inhabitants thereof are as grasshoppers". The conception of Israel's special relationship to God was likewise transformed. As the surrounding nations had a place in God's purposes, it came to be seen that Israel was not the chief recipient of God's favours for its own sake, but had to perform the function of spreading the knowledge of God and of his demands among the nations. Thus there grew up the conception of all mankind as forming a single great society, and of Israel as having a function to perform within this society. In so far as this conception was accepted, it removed the sense of the isolation of the society of Israel from other societies. Unfortunately the conception did not take very firm root, and older and more imperfect conceptions continued along with it.

This was roughly the position when in the Hellenistic age the Jewish people had to meet the challenge of Hellenistic culture. Some were attracted by it, and the people as a whole might easily have become assimilated to the surrounding peoples and lost their identity. There was a strong reaction, however. Observance of the Law was insisted on, with special emphasis on those practices which increased the separateness of the Jews, such as the keeping of the Sabbath. This was probably a sound course to adopt at the time, in order to avert the risk of assimilation and the loss of Israel's distinctive religious insights. By the time of Jesus, however, Palestine had been incorporated in the Roman empire, and the need was for emphasis on the function of Israel as teacher of the surrounding peoples. Instead of this, earlier ideas of the special relationship of Israel to God had developed into a largely secular nationalism, and a neurotic application of the belief that God would always support his chosen people was leading to a collision with Rome. The collision actually took place in two stages in the risings of A.D. 67-70 and 121, and these had disastrous consequences for the Jews.

This inflation of the Jewish group-consciousness was supported not only by the mainly secular Sadducees but also by the devout and religious-minded Pharisees. In the latter it was combined with an inflation of the ego-consciousness. The Pharisees had elaborated the tradition of scrupulously observing the Law. For one thing this made it very difficult for the devout Jew to have contacts with non-Jews. It also encouraged him to compare his observance of the Law with that of other Jews, and to pride himself on his achievements in this respect. The emphasis came to be on the external aspect of the Law and not on its spirit, and a high degree of fulfilment, or even perfect fulfilment, became possible for those who had sufficient time, money, or enthusiasm. The gospels admittedly present the case against the Pharisees; but, even when every allowance is made for the defence that could be made from their standpoint, it would seem that the form of piety which had grown up among them was ministering to a serious inflation of the ego-consciousness or, in ordinary language, to spiritual pride.

Such was the state of affairs in the early years of the Christian era, and it might well occasion profound despair in the heart of any sincere and devout Jew. There were not merely the ever-present grounds for hopelessness—false valuations and neurotic tendencies, and the perpetuation of these by heredity and environment. Worse than that, the curative forces which had been

D   41

at work in Israel for centuries had become corrupt at their very centre; and meanwhile pilotless Israel was drifting towards collision with Rome. The salt of the religious leadership had lost its saltness; how could it be resalted? Even if a new prophet appeared, could he cure this infection at the very heart of the religious life of Israel? God had been at work in Israel for centuries, attempting to heal their wounds; but now the curative forces had themselves become diseased. Would not the same happen to any fresh curative forces which appeared? The situation was gloomy—indeed, quite literally, hopeless.

2 THE MISSION OF JESUS

The preparatory movement

The spiritual revival whose centre was John the Baptist may be regarded as preparatory to that of Jesus. Jesus himself was baptized by John, and after John's death many of those influenced by his revival became followers of Jesus. A few remained independent of the Christian community for several years after the crucifixion, but in the end all were probably absorbed; at least the Baptist's movement ceased to exist as such.

Various notes may be distinguished in the teaching of John the Baptist as it is recorded in the gospels (Luke 3. 1-18; Mark 1. 4-11; Matt. 3). First, there is a return from the formal and external morality of the Pharisees to the fundamental moral concepts emphasized by the Old Testament prophets, such as justice, upright dealing, truthfulness, and generosity. This was not merely a deepening of morality; it had social implications. The morality of the Pharisees was such that the community of the faithful worshippers of God tended to shut themselves off from the rest of the world, since close contacts with other people led to ritual uncleanness and necessitated an elaborate and cumbersome ritual purification. Even for most Jews this was impossible; they ceased to try to keep themselves ritually pure, and were classed by the strict upholders of the law as "sinners". The insistence on the fundamental moral virtues meant that the new morality preached by John was suited to a cosmopolitan society, in which men inevitably had contacts with members of other faiths. By saying nothing about ritual uncleanness, John tacitly implied that it was unimportant. At the same time he spoke of God's moral demands even on those like tax-collectors and soldiers who were in contact with non-Jews, and gave them the hope that if they fulfilled these moral demands they might face God's judgement with confidence.

A second note in John's teaching was his call for repentance. This was closely connected, of course, with his insistence on the moral virtues. He taught, moreover, that repentance was urgent because judgement was imminent—as he put it, the axe was already being laid at the roots of the trees to cut down the unsatisfactory ones. We cannot be certain from the scanty records whether he thought of this judgement as occurring in historical time, or at the end of the world. He possibly laid the main emphasis on a judgement in history, involved in the threatened collision with Rome, but at the same time did not clearly distinguish from this the idea of eschatological judgement, and so did not exclude it. With repentance John connected the rite of baptism, and from this special feature came to be known as the Baptist. The outward sign or seal of repentance was baptism, that is, immersion in the river Jordan, and the rite was conducted by John or one of his disciples. The underlying idea was presumably that the stains caused by moral imperfections in the past were washed away. This baptism of repentance was well adapted to the needs of the time. In so far as Pharisees availed themselves of it, it counteracted the inflation of their ego-consciousness, and made possible a healthier attitude to life. For those who had hitherto been classed as "sinners", and who had probably been in despair because of the impossibility of keeping the Law properly, it brought hope, for they were now able to think of themselves as having a place in the purposes of God.

Thirdly, John tried to deal with the inflation of the group-consciousness. He warned his hearers that it was not sufficient to rely on Israel's special relation to God, and that they must not assume that all would be well with them because they were physical descendants of Abraham. On the contrary, if they would face God with confidence, they must "bring forth fruits worthy of repentance", that is, fulfil God's moral demands. In other words, John was attacking the false conception of Israel's special relationship to God, and insisting that it was not a privilege to be enjoyed, which brought no corresponding duties; rather all relationship to God involved responsibility for the quality of one's conduct.

What we are told about John is very little. He may well have mentioned other points that would be relevant to the present study, but there is no mention of them. Sufficient is told us, however, to show us that he was aware of the inflated group-consciousness and the inflated ego-consciousness of his time, and was trying to correct what was wrong. While he may not have said anything explicitly about the function of the Jews with regard to other peoples, he was thinking of individual Jews as members of the cosmopolitan society of the Roman empire, and he was laying down the basic principles for the morality necessary for such a society.

The early work of Jesus

The beginnings of the preaching of Jesus followed closely on that of John the Baptist. The gospels make much of John's announcement that he would be followed by someone greater than himself and his identification of this person with Jesus. In view of subsequent events, these matters are no doubt given an emphasis in the gospel records that is out of all proportion to the place they occupied in John's preaching; perhaps most of his hearers hardly noticed them at the time. This is no reason, however, to doubt their authenticity, or the close connection of the work of Jesus with that of John the Baptist.

The early preaching of Jesus contained the notes that were

present in the preaching of John. He called on men to repent, and, sometimes at least, made baptism accompany repentance (e.g. Mark 1. 15; John 3. 22). From this call to repentance we may infer that from the first he gave moral teaching similar to that of John, and this inference is amply borne out by the records of his ministry and of his attacks on the formal morality of the Pharisees and their neglect of the basic virtues like justice and mercy (Matt. 23, esp. v. 23). In the Sermon on the Mount, for example, he asserts as demands of God not merely that men should refrain from committing murder and adultery, but that they should not entertain in their hearts the thoughts which lead to these sins (Matt. 5. 21-30). A whole chapter in the first gospel is devoted to his criticisms of the scribes and Pharisees, while in the third gospel, the story of the Pharisee and the tax-collector who went up into the temple to pray, pillories the inflated ego-consciousness of the former; his prayer was one of thanksgiving for his superiority to other men through his observance of the Law, whereas the tax-collector simply said "God be merciful to me as a sinner", but it was the tax-collector whom Jesus declared to be justified (Matt. 23; Luke 18. 9-14).

In one respect it appears that from the first the teaching of Jesus went beyond that of John the Baptist. John had called men to repent because judgement was imminent. Jesus proclaimed that the "kingdom (or rule) of God" was at hand, and, while this included judgement, the emphasis was more on a positive aspect—the putting right of what was wrong. This is, of course, no more than a preliminary description of a conception of great complexity. The total achievement of Jesus might be said to be summed up in the phrase, "the establishment of the rule of God"; and the attempt to describe this achievement in modern terms will occupy the next section of this book. Meanwhile let us use the phrase without further examining its meaning. The coming of the kingdom of God properly has a central place in the teaching of Jesus. He proclaims that the fulfilment of the prophecies about the kingdom has already begun. The acts of healing he performed, and the various other works usually

45

called "miracles", were chiefly important as "signs" of the kingdom. While the kingdom is thus already present, it has also a future aspect. The prophecies have begun to be fulfilled, but they were completely fulfilled only in the climax of the ministry of Jesus. There is still a sense, too, in which Christians believe that they may properly pray for the coming of God's kingdom.

Of the notes mentioned above as present in the teaching of John the Baptist, the third was related to the inflated group-consciousness of Israel, and this note likewise is repeated by Jesus. It is not prominent in extent in the records of his teaching, but it has a fundamental place, for it is implied in his assertions about judgement, and therefore in his assertions about the coming of the kingdom of God. Because the Jews have not fulfilled God's demands on them, they will be excluded from his kingdom, while many strangers will come to share in its privileges. The point was made in various forms. There was the story of men who asked to be admitted after the master of the house had shut the door, and who were refused and addressed as "workers of iniquity"; "ye shall see Abraham and Isaac and Jacob, and all the prophets, in the kingdom of God, and you yourselves thrust out; and they shall come from the east, and from the west, and from the north, and from the south, and shall sit down in the kingdom of God" (Luke 13. 28 f.). When a centurion, who was of course not a Jew, believed so entirely in Jesus that he considered him able to heal a sick man at a distance without seeing him, this was seen as an exemplification, or at least a premonition, of the entry of non-Jews into God's kingdom (Matt. 8. 5-13). More and more towards the end of his ministry did Jesus dwell on his rejection by the Jews and on their replacement by other people. For example, in the parable of the vineyard (Mark 12. 1 ff.; Matt. 21. 33 ff.; Luke 20. 9 ff.), the men to whom the owner had let it, but who had proved unsatisfactory, were driven out, and it was let to others instead of them. Thus the development which had been dimly foreseen by John the Baptist was at hand; and subsequent events showed that the function of communicating the knowledge of God to the surrounding peoples had in fact passed from the Jews to the new people of God, the new Israel, namely, the Christian Church.

There is no contradiction between this warning that the Jews will be replaced and the restriction to Jews of the mission of Jesus and his disciples. Jesus occasionally had contacts with non-Jews, but these were exceptional, and in connection with one of them he is reported to have said, "I am not sent but unto the lost sheep of the house of Israel" (Matt. 15. 24; cf. 10. 5 f.). This concentration on the Jews was what the situation required. In a sense Israel was performing its function of sharing its knowledge of God with others; even the Pharisees were missionary-minded and would "compass sea and land" to make one convert. The trouble was that Israel was corrupt at the centre; it was salt that had lost its saltness. The corruption of the missionaries was increased in the converts. The corruption at the centre was thus of chief importance and needed to be tackled first. Otherwise there could be no healthy expansion. Moreover, an attempt at this period to preach regularly to non-Jews would have been seized upon by opponents as a betrayal of Israel and even of Israel's religion, and would have led to entanglement in secondary issues. On various grounds, then, it was necessary that Israel should first be given an opportunity of spiritual renewal.

The conflict with evil

The whole of the ministry of Jesus, like that of John the Baptist before him, was an attempt to deal with the evil that had poisoned the life of Israel at its source. The call to repentance implied that something was wrong, and all the teaching was an implicit criticism of aspects of the existing situation. In the later stages of the ministry of Jesus, however, the conflict with the forces of evil came more to the surface, and may thus be regarded as specially characterizing this period.

The chief opponents of Jesus at first appear to have been the Pharisees, in conjunction with the "scribes" or canon-lawyers. Sometimes when Jesus was dealing with a sick man he would say "Thy sins are forgiven"; and this was criticized by the scribes and Pharisees as a claim to do something which only God could do. They criticized him also for allowing the breaking of the regulations about doing no work on the Sabbath. If his disciples plucked ears of corn on the Sabbath to relieve their hunger, that was work; and if on the Sabbath Jesus told a man whom he had just cured of paralysis to lift up his pallet and go home, he was ordering him to do work. In these ways, they urged, Jesus was failing to insist on the observance of the Law. Moreover, when he associated with tax-collectors and "sinners", he was mixing with people who failed to observe the Law, and mostly did not even try to do so. Consequently, his conduct fell far below the standards required by the Pharisees. Since the inveterate Pharisees thus necessarily regarded Jesus as a "sinner", it was unthinkable for them that his acts of healing should be manifestations of power from God (cf. John 9. 16). Some therefore suggested that he achieved his cures through evil powers—through "Beelzebul, the prince of the devils", who was supposed to have possessed him (Mark 3. 20 ff.; Matt. 12. 21 ff.; Luke 11. 14 ff.).

These verbal criticisms of Jesus by the Pharisees did not remain unanswered. The answer to the charge that he fell below the standards of the Pharisees was his call to his hearers to attain higher standards; "except your righteousness shall exceed the righteousness of the scribes and Pharisees, ye shall in no case enter into the kingdom of heaven" (Matt. 5. 20). The higher standards included such things as uprightness in thought, in contrast to the purely external observances in which the morality of the Pharisees consisted. Some of his explicit criticisms of the Pharisees are collected in one of the less familiar chapters of the first gospel (23). Pharisees, he says, are concerned with outward honour and with the outward appearance of righteousness, but within they are full of hypocrisy and all kinds of evil. They pride themselves on their religious achievements, but actually they both fail to enter the kingdom of heaven themselves and also hinder those who are entering. They are thus largely responsible for the rejection of Jesus by the Jews and for the resulting catastrophe of the nation.

The Pharisees were not the only group among the Jews who were hostile to Jesus. The scribes and Pharisees, who are often mentioned together, may be said to constitute the "intellectuals" of the time. There were also the Sadducees, who included the high-priestly family that for the moment was responsible (in subordination to the Romans) for much of the administration. It was primarily the Sadducees who brought about the crucifixion of Jesus. Besides these two groups there were the masses of the common people, who were doubtless of several different outlooks. Many of them had thronged to hear John the Baptist and Jesus, and at least some of these had been deeply influenced. The strongest feeling in most, however, was probably a nationalism with a religious tone; and it was easy for skilled orators, by playing on these feelings, to rouse the mob. In this total situation the opposition of the Pharisees to Jesus was the more serious. Had they not opposed him, the course of events would have been very different; he might conceivably have been able to carry the mass of the people with him in spite of the opposition of the Sadducees. With the Pharisees hostile, however, he could effect no fundamental change in the attitudes of the nation as a whole that would have been sufficient to avert the catastrophic clash with Rome.

Seen in this light, the conflict between Jesus and the Pharisees is the most important part of his conflict with the Jews. The essence of the conflict was, on the one side, that Jesus claimed to speak and to act with the authority of God, and, on the other side, that the Pharisees in their religious pride thought that they alone, because they alone fulfilled the Law (in their view), were able to understand and interpret what God had revealed to Moses of his nature and his demands from men.

This is clearly brought out in many passages in the fourth gospel, such as the following:

> Jesus said unto them, If ye were blind, ye should have no sin: but now ye say, We see; therefore your sin remaineth . . .
> Ye have neither heard his (God's) voice at any time, nor seen his shape. And ye have not his word abiding in you: for whom he hath sent, him ye believe not (John 9. 41, 5, 37 f.; cf. 8. 40, 46 f.).

Thus the root of the opposition to Jesus was the inflated group-consciousness of the Jews, and particularly of the scribes and Pharisees; and this inflation was itself based on what God had done in the past to cure the troubles of Israel. The medicine had apparently caused a worse disease.

With the knowledge that the "intellectuals" of the nation were opposed to Jesus, the Sadducees proceeded to use force against him. He was threatened with arrest or violent death if he preached publicly in Judaea (e.g. John 7. 1, 30; 11. 8). Because of this his public ministry was now confined to Galilee (which was under a different administration), apart from a brief and partly secret visit to Judaea at the time of the feast of tabernacles. This curtailment of the activities of Jesus placed him in a difficult situation and led to the climax of his career. To accept the limitation of his sphere of influence dictated by his opponents would be tantamount to abandoning the task he had undertaken. He might be able to continue preaching in Galilee for some years or at least months, but the chances were that the opposition would close Galilee to him also. In that case his best course of action would be to leave Palestine and go to the Jews of the Dispersion scattered in groups in the cities of the Roman Empire. This course, which was the chief alternative to that of challenging his opponents, is hinted at in the New Testament (cf. John 7. 35).

We cannot hope to see the choice before Jesus as he saw it, but we can understand some of the factors involved. By going to the Dispersion and preaching in all probability for many years, he might hope to secure numerous followers and to inaugurate a vast spiritual movement. Nevertheless, however strong this movement became in numbers, it would always have a fundamental weakness. At the back of its consciousness there would be the knowledge that its founder had been deflected from his course by forces of blindness and prejudice; and this would imply that these forces were stronger than those produced by genuine religious enthusiasm. Moreover, the fundamental problem of the corruption of the curative influences would not have been solved. For Jesus to have gone to preach to the Dispersion, then, would not have been satisfactory. It might have had some partial and temporary successes, but essentially it would have been the admission of defeat.

The course which Jesus chose was that of confronting his opponents openly and challenging them to do their worst. There are several points to be noticed specially. The first is that Jesus was careful to make his challenge an open and public one. He knew that John the Baptist had died as a protest against evil; but he had died in a hidden fashion, not in such a way as to inspire to further action the crowds who had been impressed by his preaching. Jesus, therefore, did not slip into Jerusalem unobserved as he had done on a previous occasion. He made a triumphal entry, with crowds throwing palm branches and garments in front of him as he rode, and shouting an enthusiastic welcome. For several days he publicly addressed the people in the Temple. His actions thus constituted so public a challenge to his opponents that they could not ignore it.

That Jesus was able to act in this way is at first sight surprising, but can readily be explained. The Jewish authorities were either unable, or unwilling, to arrest him in the presence of the crowd. They had tried to do so on a previous occasion (at the feast of tabernacles), but their agents were too impressed by his personality, as they themselves claimed, and perhaps also too afraid of the crowd, to carry out their orders. An arrest, if it could have been made at all, would have led to serious disorders and might have embroiled them with their Roman superiors. The Jewish authorities therefore decided that Jesus must be arrested when there was no crowd present. Jesus, however, was careful, so long as it suited him, to give them no opportunities of taking him prisoner. He spent the nights outside Jerusalem at Bethany, where he was presumably among friends and would have had warning of any attempt to capture him. In the crowds who had come to Jerusalem for the passover festival it was doubtless easy to slip into and out of the Temple unobserved. Arrest only became possible when Judas, one of Jesus' closest followers, betrayed his retreat to the authorities.

Under these circumstances, an obvious line for the opponents of Jesus to try was to endeavour to undermine his influence with the crowds. Groups of men were sent to ask him awkward questions, which it would be difficult for him to answer without giving them an opportunity of rousing the crowd against him. The initiative probably came from the party of the high-priest, the Sadducees, but the scribes and Pharisees, or at least some of them, helped to constitute the groups. One of their questions was "by what authority" he acted as he did. Another was about the legality of paying tribute to Rome. Jesus not merely parried these questions without losing face with the crowd, but in turn asked others which led to the humiliation of his opponents. In particular he asked how the Messiah could be the son of David when in one of the Psalms of David (110), which was admittedly messianic, he was referred to as "my Lord".

These questions involve the second point of note about the conduct of Jesus during the last week. He took pains to ensure that the conflict between him and the leaders of the Jews should be focussed on the central issue, and that he should not die for something secondary and incidental. Had he said, in reply to the first question, that he was acting by the authority of God, he might have been challenged to lead a rising against Rome. The Jews were expecting a Messiah who would make them victorious over their national enemies; but this expectation was an expression of that very inflation of the group-consciousness which Jesus was attempting to counter. In effect the answer of Jesus was that his authority was similar to that of John the Baptist; in this way he did not deny that he was sent by God, yet he made it clear that he was not the military leader who was expected. Again, in dealing with the legality of tribute, he made his questioners produce a Roman coin, and thereby compromised them in the eyes of the crowd. His reply, "Render unto Caesar the things that are Caesar's and unto God the things that are God's", might be taken to mean that tribute was legal (by God's law) so long as the Jews were subject to the Romans and enjoying the benefits of the *pax Romana*; it avoided any declaration of war against Rome in the immediate future, without excluding the possibility of a holy war at some future date; but against the background of the teaching of Jesus as a whole, it meant that in claiming to be the Messiah he was chiefly concerned with bringing the Jews to God, either in repentance or for judgement.

The resolve of Jesus to focus attention on the central issue between himself and his opponents also explains his silence during his trial. To have answered questions about conspiring to destroy the Temple would have been a distraction. When, however, the high priest asked him directly whether he was "the Christ (Messiah), the son of the Blessed", he replied that he was, and that they would "see the Son of Man sitting at the right hand of Power and coming on the clouds of heaven". He thus claimed a special commission from God, but not (apparently) a political one. This was the fundamental issue. The Jewish authorities decided that his claim was blasphemy and that he was liable to death. Thus the decision that led to the death of Jesus was a decision on the fundamental issue. To this extent Jesus had had his way.

This brings us to the third point of note about the last days of his ministry. Considering that powerful enemies were seeking the life of Jesus, he managed to exercise a wide control over the course of events. He secured that his condemnation should be on the fundamental issue. He also largely controlled the timing of events. He must have deliberately chosen that the climax of his ministry should coincide with the passover festival, since he was trying to do something that was a completion of that deliverance of Israel commemorated in the passover. He also appears to have wanted his death to happen as nearly as possible at the same time as the killing of the lambs for the festival meal. The meal was eaten on the fifteenth of the Jewish month of Nisan, which in this year fell on the Sabbath (that is, the period of twenty-four hours from sunset on Friday to sunset on Saturday); in this year, then, the passover meal would be on Friday evening by modern reckoning. Before he was separated from them, Jesus wanted to have some time with his disciples. In the rush of public addresses and disputes there could have been little time for private converse, and he had to explain to them, so far as they could understand it, the significance of what he was doing. He therefore made secret arrangements for a meal on Thursday evening, and only after that gave his opponents an opportunity of arresting him through the traitor Judas.

The fourth and last point to be noted here is that Jesus paid careful attention to the significance or symbolic character of what he was doing, even in its details. (I shall later have to discuss the meaning of "the significance or symbolic character" of actions, and therefore for the moment leave the phrase without further explanation, as a vague indication of what is intended.) Not merely was the climax of his ministry made to coincide with the passover festival as a whole, but his own death took place nearly at the same time as the sacrifice of the passover lamb. For his triumphal entry into Jerusalem he chose to ride on an ass, presumably in order to show that he was not the victorious military leader commonly expected as Messiah, but the peaceful king depicted by the prophet Zechariah (9. 9). At his last meal with his disciples, Jesus, in full realization of his central place in human history, insisted on performing the servile act of washing their feet. Finally, at this same meal he took bread and wine, associated them with his body and blood about to be sacrificed, broke the bread, and distributed the bread and wine to those present. It was a symbolic act, and, probably as

Jesus intended, has been adopted by his followers as the supreme symbol of what he did for them. Thus the whole activity of Jesus at the climax of his ministry has a symbolic character, and this is by no means the least important aspect of the events.

After the last meal with the disciples Jesus went with them a little way outside the city to the garden of Gethsemane. To this spot Judas led a mixed body of men belonging to the Jewish authorities, and Jesus was arrested. He was immediately tried by the high priest and sentenced to death, and the sentence was ratified by the Roman governor, Pontius Pilate, and without delay carried out by a squad of Roman soldiers. The method of execution was the painful one of crucifixion. Jesus hung on the cross, conscious, for several hours, occasionally speaking words that showed that he was still thinking of the symbolic character of what was happening. Towards the middle of the afternoon he died, and some friends obtained leave from the Roman authorities to remove his body. It was hastily placed in a near-by tomb as a temporary resting-place, since with the beginning of the Sabbath at sunset all work had to cease. The Sabbath ended at sunset on the Saturday, but nothing could be done after dark. It was therefore not until early on Sunday morning that some women followers went to the tomb to prepare the body for permanent burial. To their surprise, they found the heavy stone rolled away from the entrance of the tomb, and the tomb empty.

What had happened between Friday afternoon and Sunday morning? What happened afterwards in the fifty days until Pentecost? There is much in the records that is puzzling, and much that we should like to have in them is absent. We in the twentieth century are factually and materially minded, but the writers of the records were not interested in bare facts, but only in significant facts, and they write in such a way that it is often impossible for us to analyse their significant facts into bare facts on the one hand, and the significance of these facts on the other. Consequently many of the questions we should like to ask about

55

bare facts have to remain unanswered. We cannot, for example, give a scientific account of what happened to the body of Jesus. On the other hand, there is one big certainty. That is that the followers of Jesus became convinced that the conclusion of his ministry, which to all appearance was a defeat, was in fact a victory. This conviction led, some seven weeks after the morning when the tomb was found empty, to a great outburst of libidinal energy. This outburst of energy in its turn has had consequences which bulk large in the history of mankind as a whole. These are bare facts which cannot reasonably be doubted.

A certainty of minor import is that the body of Jesus somehow disappeared between Friday afternoon and Sunday morning, and that nobody alive in the weeks, months, and years after Pentecost knew the whereabouts of any tomb or grave containing the body. The grounds for this statement are inferential, but they seem to be inexpugnable. Briefly, the argument is as follows. The followers of Jesus could not have moved the body, since, if they knew where it lay mouldering in a grave, they would have had no reason for suffering persecution and death in their preaching of Jesus as risen from the dead. Neither Jews nor Romans could have moved the body, since both were opposed to Christian teaching, and, in order to refute it, would have produced the body if they could, That really exhausts the possibilities, apart from Judas. Could Judas in a fit of madness have done something with the body and then died without telling anyone? It is almost certain that this was impossible since the weight of the stone closing the tomb would be such that one man could not remove it unaided. Thus, while it may be possible to frame hypotheses about the removal of the body that cannot apodictically be proved impossible, no such hypothesis is in the least degree credible. The only reasonable attitudes are acceptance of the orthodox Christian view, or admission of complete ignorance about what happened to the body.

Any unorthodox hypothesis about the removal of the body would be entirely on the physical plane. The orthodox view, on the other hand, is not restricted to the physical plane, but moves into the plane of the meaningful or significant. According to the orthodox view, the body of Jesus which was restored to life appeared on several occasions to his followers. It was physical to the extent that Thomas was able to touch the marks of the wounds made by crucifixion; but it could also apparently pass through closed doors and disappear in an instant. Finally, on the fortieth day, Jesus, that is, his body, disappeared from his disciples skyward, and they came to believe that he was seated at the right hand of God. Now this process of the body from the tomb to the right hand of God is not entirely a physical, or physically observable, process. The placing of the body in the tomb is clearly physical, and the sitting on the right hand of God is as clearly not physical. The belief of the first Christians in the resurrection and ascension of Jesus, though belonging essentially to the plane of the meaningful, had a physical basis; but from the data they have left to us it is impossible to say how extensive was the physical basis.

There is a sense in which the resurrection and ascension of Jesus belong not so much to his own history as to that of his followers. These events mark stages in their understanding of his achievement. So far as he himself was concerned, his work had been brought to a successful conclusion with the cry from the cross of *tetelestai*, "it is finished, completed, consummated". The Christian of to-day, with his sophistication and his interest in the physical and material, has to learn to accept naïvely the assertions of the first Christians about the resurrection and ascension without attempting to abstract the physical basis from the total event as it is described to us. Yet if, with regard to the resurrection and ascension, he is unable to look at the physical facts for himself and form his own estimate of their significance, nevertheless for the events leading up to the crucifixion and the cry of *tetelestai* he has adequate material. Moreover, it is here that the primary question lies, namely, whether in essentials Jesus gave to men a cure for all their troubles. When this question is answered in the affirmative, the traditional accounts of the resurrection and ascension are seen to be congruent.

E   57

In the present section an outline of the facts of the ministry of Jesus has been given with a minimum of interpretation. In the next section I shall try to show how Jesus through what he did, said, and allowed to be done to him, effected a cure for human troubles.

3 THE ACHIEVEMENT OF JESUS

To speak of the achievement of Jesus is to speak about the greatest subject with which man deals, and also the most difficult. The difficulties are twofold. Some arise from the profundity and richness of the subject; it reaches down to the depths of human experience and has greater width and variety than can be comprehended in a single life. Other difficulties are due to the fact that the subject can only be spoken about in pictures, that is, in terms of concepts which, like pictures or maps, present to us certain aspects of the realities adequately enough for various practical purposes, though they are far from being replicas of the realities in their totality. I shall therefore first attempt to depict the achievement of Jesus in terms of modern concepts, and afterwards consider the relation of what has been said to the chief traditional pictures.

A modern statement

Since the work of Jesus, Christians assert, is to provide in essence the cure for human troubles, it must be relevant to these troubles in accordance with the analysis of them given above. The source to which they were traced was the appearance of self-consciousness, first as a group-consciousness, then as ego-consciousness. As the group or individual becomes more aware of its distinct existence, it loses its awareness of its relatedness or partnership with other groups or individuals, and also its awareness of its place in the universe as a whole and its dependence on the principle of integration of the universe, God. These losses of awareness produce a feeling of weakness, insecurity and isolation, and to counteract them there is an inflation of self-consciousness, that is, the belief grows up that the self is better, stronger and more important than it really is. At the same time, because of its inadequate picture of the universe and of its own place in it, the self comes to accept false or partial values. Thus it fails to understand the place of suffering and death in the scheme of things, so that they appear to it more terrible and destructive than they really are. Such acceptance of false values, and the accompanying inability to appreciate and accept true values, constitute neurosis, so that in a sense all men are suffering from neurosis, though the term is usually restricted to some specially acute cases.

The curative work of God in the Old Testament period is relevant to most of the aspects of human troubles just mentioned. The loss of the sense of community with other groups is not dealt with directly, but knowledge is attained of the dependence of the group on God, and on that basis there is a partial recognition that Israel shares a common life with other societies. The knowledge that the group is dependent on God likewise reduces its feeling of insecurity and isolation, and the inflation of the group-consciousness is corrected by the insistence of the prophets that God makes demands and that Israel has failed to fulfil these demands. The message of the prophets, and previously that of Moses, involved the presentation of true values; and these were presented in such a way and in such a context (the activity of God in history, as when he delivered Israel from Egypt) that they won general acceptance. That true views and true values were accepted and that past faults were likewise admitted, meant that to that extent the neurotic tendency was remedied. In the Old Testament period the main concern was with the group and not the individual, since the growth of ego-consciousness in individuals appears to have been slight; but knowledge of God's nature and of his demands would also benefit the individual.

The cure, of course, was never complete. Israel never became morally perfect. Even if (as the Christian may perhaps admit)

Israel was cured in essence, and its troubles began slowly to be cleared up, yet they were widely spread and deep-seated; false attitudes had been passed on from generation to generation. Before the cure could be applied in every particular, a new and more serious form of the disease had appeared. The healing powers operative in Israel appeared themselves to have become corrupted and to be producing disease rather than health. Knowledge of Israel's special relation to God was now increasing inflation of the group-consciousness instead of reducing it. Knowledge of God's demands was similarly inflating the ego-consciousness (in the Pharisees). What had happened was that the knowledge of God had become falsified, and with it the appreciation of values. In many people this had led to a false confidence in the political victory of Israel or in their own moral achievements. Others—those put outside the pale as "sinners"—were in despair through ignorance of the true nature of God. In many respects neurotic tendencies were increasing.

This was the particular situation in Israel when Jesus was growing up, but this situation has features which are of general relevance. It shows that a curative process, begun by the initiative of God, may go wrong. Not merely does man apart from God go wrong; man helped by God also goes wrong. In this there is one of the chief differences between the cure for human troubles as given in the Old Testament, and that in the New Testament. The Old Testament cure is for the disease of those who are still for the most part without help from God. Its focus is the Mosaic dispensation and God's deliverance of Israel from Egypt. The great prophets of the Old Testament certainly were dealing with the troubles of those who had received much help from God, but their affirmation of the action of God in contemporary history was not so influential in forming the outlook of the nation as a whole as had been the deliverance from Egypt under Moses.

The work of Jesus, then, must be relevant to the complex of troubles arising from the appearance of self-consciousness, and this complex includes the fact that curative processes sometimes lead to a more serious disease. The cure effected in essence by Jesus is similar to that effected in the Old Testament, since his teaching is based on that of Moses and the prophets. The achievement of Jesus goes beyond the achievements of the Old Testament period chiefly in two respects. One, as just indicated, is that he pays more attention to the problem of the relapse of the patient who is in the process of being cured, or, in other words, the nation or individual who, after being helped by God to overcome sin, falls once more into sin. The other respect is that the work of Jesus is more fully adapted to the needs of the individual. The needs of the community are not neglected in the New Testament, nor are those of the individual absent from the Old Testament. Nevertheless, the individual has a centrality in the New Testament that he has not in the Old. The individualistic aspect was already marked in Jeremiah's vision of the "new covenant" (31. 29-34):

> In those days they shall say no more, The fathers have eaten a sour grape, and the children's teeth are set on edge. But every one shall die for his own iniquity; every man that eateth the sour grape, his teeth shall be set on edge.
> Behold the days come, saith the Lord, that I will make a new covenant with the house of Israel, and with the house of Judah . . . After those days, saith the Lord, I will put my law in their inward parts, and write it in their hearts; and will be their God and they shall be my people. And they shall teach no more every man his neighbour, and every man his brother, saying, Know the Lord: for they shall all know me, from the least of them unto the greatest of them . . .

A large part of the achievement of Jesus was that, through his teaching, he gave men a fuller revelation of the nature of God. He reaffirmed and developed the truths that had been asserted by Moses and the prophets. Thus he reiterated, and even heightened, God's ethical demands upon men. God's standard, he taught, was not merely higher than that of the scribes and Pharisees, whose morality was formal and restricted, and who sometimes approved of outward actions that were contrary to the great moral virtues. God demanded moral excellence in thought as well as in outward act. Moreover, this new standard was not set as a distant goal towards which men were to aspire; if they failed to fulfil God's demands, he would condemn and punish them.

Such teaching by itself would have led to despair, but it was balanced by a greater insistence on God's love for men, on his readiness to forgive them when they acknowledged their sins, and on his initiative in helping them before they asked for his help. Taken together, the two sides of the teaching of Jesus offered a conception of the universe and of God which, if accepted, was a remedy for the troubles arising from the appearance of self-consciousness. The high moral demands on a man, and the acknowledgement of his sin, led to a deflation of his inflated ego-consciousness, or a humiliation of his pride. At the same time, the knowledge of God's forgiving love tended to remove the feeling of isolation and insecurity. As man gained, or regained, awareness of his relationship to God, he also gained, or regained, awareness of his partnership with other men in the business of living; and thus the grounds of the inflation of self-consciousness were gradually removed. Against this background Jesus also taught something of the place of suffering and death in God's purposes (thus countering the effects of the Fall); but what he said on this subject made less impression on his followers than what he did. This brings us to the second and most important part of the achievement of Jesus.

Teaching about the nature of God and his demands from men is only effective in curing them in so far as they accept it. To accept this teaching, too, means not merely to be convinced of its truth, but to desire from the depths of one's being to fulfil God's demands—to love him with heart and soul and mind and strength. A merely verbal and intellectual presentation of the message is unlikely to produce this attitude in a man. It must be presented in such a form and such a setting that it provokes a response from the depths in him. False valuation and neurotic tendencies are deeply-rooted in men. If these are to be changed and cured, the men must be thoroughly roused or deeply stirred, so that power is made available in them to effect the change. The second and greatest part of the achievement of Jesus was that by his actions, even more than by his words, he presented truths about God and man in a form which stirred them to the depths. He revived, in the language of C. G. Jung, "archetypes of the collective unconscious", "primordial images" that lie near the centre of man's being. This revival of archetypes led in its turn, in those men and women in whom it was effective, to the release of libidinal energy which brought about the expansion of the Christian Church. It is not possible for us to explain how this release of energy comes about. We can at most reach a partial understanding of certain aspects by considering them in greater detail.

The most important thing to notice is that Jesus was deliberately moulding his life and activity so that it exhibited certain archetypes, or rather a synthesis of archetypal patterns. His immediate concern, of course, was with the archetypes in the particular forms in which they had been clothed in the experience of Israel. Thus he claimed to be the divine hero expected by Israel, the Messiah. He established a parallel between what he was doing and God's deliverance of Israel through the instrumentality of Moses. In his acceptance of suffering he lived out Isaiah's picture of the suffering servant. In this living out of archetypes or images, however, he was not simply trying to recover the past; he was effecting a creative synthesis of selected images. While claiming to be the Messiah, he rejected the image of a victorious war-leader. Instead, in his triumphal entry into Jerusalem he copied the features of the mild and gentle Messiah described by Zechariah; and with the picture of the Messiah he fused that of the suffering servant, which would seem to have been originally applied to Israel as a whole. Altogether, then, his life—and especially his passion and death— embodied many of the traditional images of Israel's experience. It is not surprising, therefore, that it called forth a dynamic and revolutionary response.

Just as Jesus taught that God took the initiative in his dealings with men, so his activity, he asserted, was due not to any individual initiative of his own, but to the initiative of God the Father. Invoking one of the traditional images of God's relationship to his people, he spoke of himself as the good shepherd, and he went in search of the lost sheep of the house of Israel. In this way his life exemplified the prevenient love of God. Moreover, because in the activity of Jesus the initiative was God's, opposition to Jesus was opposition to God, and the passion and death of Jesus becomes an embodiment of the consequences of man's sin. The climax and consummation of the activity of Jesus was the cross on which he died, and the cross thus comes to epitomize both the destructiveness of sin and the prevenience of God's love, and to produce both humiliation of man's self-consciousness, and confidence in his association with God and with the rest of the universe.

The activity of Jesus is also a demonstration of the superiority of the forces through which the Divine initiative works itself out to the forces that oppose it. The miracles of Jesus are evidences of God's power to heal and transform human life. Above all his death is a victory, a victory over prejudice and blindness, and all the other false attitudes resulting from the appearance of self-consciousness, transmitted from generation to generation, and often becoming more fixed and more corrupt with the passage of time. On the face of it the death of Jesus is not victory but defeat; but those who have "eyes to see", when they contemplate the series of events leading to his death, find in it a meaning compared with which death is irrelevant. It was perhaps something of this sort which Jesus had in mind when he said, as Judas hastened away to betray him, "Now is the son of man glorified" (John 13. 31).

In this experience of the victoriousness, or meaningfulness, of a death, there is something mysterious. Is it any more mysterious, however, than the revival of the power of an archetype in a man? I should like to suggest that these two mysteries are two aspects of one happening; that is, the perception of meaning when contemplating archetypal events is the conscious aspect of what the observer describes as the revival of an archetype. This may seem hazardously speculative. Yet there are grounds for it. If archetypes or primordial images are somewhere near the heart of religion, and if, as I have maintained elsewhere, religion is the sphere of the meaningful or significant, then there must be a close relationship between archetypes and the meaningful. In the New Testament history, from a psychological standpoint, the resurrection and ascension of Jesus, and the outpouring of the Holy Spirit at Pentecost, mark three stages in the revival of the archetypes, or perhaps we should say, in the vitalization of the archetypal synthesis. At the resurrection and ascension the emphasis, so far as the followers of Jesus are concerned, is on the advances in their consciousness and not in their observable activity. With Pentecost, however, greater prominence is attached to outwardly observable activity. Pentecost is the release of life-energy from the vitalization of the archetypal synthesis.

From this release of libidinal or life-energy there proceed both correction of past faults and an adequate response to the present situation. The awakening of a deep level of the unconscious makes possible the cure of many of the neurotic complexes occurring at a less deep level. This cure of the festering wounds remaining from the past was aided in New Testament practice by insistence on repentance from past sins. Men were called on to repent and be baptized, that is, to be sacramentally washed, so that stains incurred in the past were removed. Along with acceptance of the teaching of Jesus, and the release of libidinal energy, went an increased ability to appreciate the true valuations included in his teaching, and a fuller understanding of the universe and therefore of the situations in which a man found himself. In this way a man became better able to respond adequately to his circumstances. Thus, through the work of Jesus, what had been wrong in men's past lives was set right for them, and in the present they were enabled to avoid going wrong again.

The archetypal synthesis present in the culminating events of the ministry of Jesus was suited to the needs of the individual as well as to those of the community. Sin, that is, failure to fulfil the demands of God, constituted the centre of the difficulties to be overcome, and sin existed both in individuals and in communities. In this way the New Testament marks an advance on the Old. In the latter, the central and archetypal experience is the deliverance of Israel from Egypt, and this is supported by the prophetic interpretations of contemporary history. These experiences, however, are those of a nation rather than of individuals. To some extent they can be applied to individuals, but there are also difficulties. A nation's prosperity or adversity can very often be correlated with its high or low moral and religious outlook. (Such a belief has in recent years been supported by Arnold Toynbee with his view that the breakdown and disintegration of a civilization is always due to internal causes.) In the case of individuals, however, so far as material prosperity is concerned, external and accidental factors may play a large part. It is probably because of this that unmerited suffering, such as that of Job, was an insoluble problem in the Old Testament period. The archetypal forms available were derived from the experience of the nation, and could not easily be applied to the experience of an individual.

It should be noted that the assertion that Jesus was deliberately living out an archetypal synthesis does not imply that he was aware of all the archetypes that later generations have found in his history or "projected" into it. The veneration of the Blessed Virgin Mary in certain parts of Christendom, whether as *Theotokos* or "Our Lady", appears to be a resuscitation of the archetype present in the worship of the Great Mother, and of this Jesus was presumably not aware. Yet he must have been to some extent aware of the archetypes present in the fertility cults since he thought of his death as a sacrifice. He could even make such a remark as, "Except a corn of wheat fall into the ground and die, it abideth alone : but if it die, it bringeth forth much fruit" (John 12. 24). Consequently it is probably not possible to draw a hard and fast line between the archetypes which

Jesus was consciously trying to live out and those of which he was not conscious.

Lastly, it may be asked whether there is any finality about the achievement of Jesus. It has to be admitted, I believe, that the Christian Church—the new Israel—is liable to corruption at its very heart in much the same way as was the old Israel. It is arguable that God will preserve it from total corruption (cf. Matt. 16. 18), but it is likewise certain that at periods in its past history parts of it have become partly corrupt. In such cases there has been sooner or later a fresh Divine initiative—human leaders have been inspired—to remove the corruption. Now let us suppose (though it may be impossible) that the Church has reached such a degree of corruption that only a leader comparable in stature to Jesus could restore it. What would be his relation to Jesus, and what would be the relation of his archetypal synthesis to that of Jesus? We cannot, of course, foresee even in our own circumstances, still less in this hypothetical case, what archetypal synthesis and what manner of its presentation would lead to a fresh release of libidinal energy. It seems clear, however, that a new archetypal synthesis of this kind would have to contain, in some form or other, most of the archetypal synthesis of Jesus, in much the same way as his synthesis contained most of the archetypal material from the Old Testament. Consequently the leader effecting this new synthesis would have to adopt some positive attitude towards the person of Jesus, because of the importance of the person of Jesus in his synthesis; and this would seem to imply that he would have to accept the claims of Jesus and regard himself as the restorer of the work of Jesus. Moreover, the development of individualism between the ages of Moses and Jesus meant that in the time of Jesus there was room for a radically new archetypal synthesis; but no development of comparable importance for religion has occurred since the time of Jesus, and therefore his archetypal synthesis and his presentation of it is still adequate and relevant to our needs. It would seem, then, that it cannot be superseded, but at most restored or reinvigorated.

The traditional accounts

The modern statement of the achievement of Jesus which has just been given differs considerably from the traditional accounts in the New Testament—later elaborations of New Testament teaching need not be considered here. It is not surprising that there should be this difference. The subject-matter is such that it can be comprehended only dimly, and only by means of images or, as I should prefer to say, pictures. Superficial contradictions between the images or pictures do not imply real contradictions, any more than the difference between an aerial photograph of a cathedral and an artist's picture painted on the ground implies a real contradiction. The achievement of Jesus is a reality with many facets, and the different pictures are of differing facets. Even within the recorded teaching of Jesus himself on the subject there is variety. For modern man the easiest path to a preliminary understanding of the achievement is a modern statement in terms of the pictures or concepts in which he normally thinks; but to advance in his understanding he must eventually go back to the words of the New Testament. This is a large task, however, and all that can be done here is to give a brief indication of connections.

A conception that is prominent in the accounts of the achievement of Jesus is that of redemption or ransom. His followers regarded him as the redeemer of the world, and he himself said that he came "to give his life a ransom for many" (Matt. 20. 28). In many parts of the Old Testament God is spoken of as redeeming his people from sin, death and adversity. To redeem is an important aspect of the activity of his protective care. The word seems to lose its precise meaning of setting free from slavery and to have the general meaning of deliverance from evil. The origin of the usage, however, is apparently God's deliverance of Israel from Egypt. Moses was commanded to

> . . . say unto the children of Israel, I am the Lord, and I will bring you out from under the burdens of the Egyptians, and I will rid you out of their bondage, and I will redeem you with a stretched out arm . . . (Ex. 6. 6).

The picture of God as redeemer was thus deeply impressed on Israel, though it was capable of having more than one interpretation in the same way as the picture of the Messiah. In so far as the achievement of Jesus is the deliverance of mankind from the sway of those forces which produce our human troubles, it is easy for a modern man to see the appropriateness of the term "redeemer" for the early Christians and to appreciate something of what they meant by it.

Another picture used by Jesus and his followers was that of sacrifice. This may indeed have been the chief thought in his phrase "a ransom for many". It lies behind his words as he took the wine at the last supper, "This is my blood of the new testament which is shed for many for the remission of sins" (Matt. 26. 26; cf. Luke 12. 20; 1 Cor. 11. 25). As has been suggested above, he appears to have acted so that his death would occur about the time of the sacrifice of the passover lamb. There is no record of him having explicitly compared himself to the sacrificial lamb, perhaps because, so long as he lived, his followers were incapable of understanding the significance of the death about which he spoke. Afterwards, however, they realized the appropriateness of the picture of the lamb. Peter wrote, "Ye were not redeemed with corruptible things . . . but with the precious blood of Christ, as of a lamb without blemish and without spot" (1 Pet. 1. 18 f.) and Paul could say, "Christ our passover is sacrificed for us" (1 Cor. 5. 7). The writer of the fourth gospel goes so far as to make John the Baptist speak of Jesus as "the Lamb of God, which taketh away the sin of the world" (John 1. 29); in view of Old Testament references (e.g. Isa. 53. 7) to the idea, this is not necessarily an anachronism, though it seems to attribute to John greater insight into the creative teaching of Jesus than one would otherwise suppose him to have; certainly the passage shows that the picture of the lamb was familiar to the early Christians. Moreover the picture of the sacrifice of Jesus was an important determinant of the ceremonial of the Eucharist.

For modern man it is very difficult to understand the

effectiveness of a sacrifice, or even of a Christian sacrament. To some extent, however, the idea of an archetype helps. To take part in a sacrifice or sacrament is to engage in an activity which is the living out of something archetypal. This living out is not creative like that of Jesus but repetitive. It is the re-enactment of an archetypal pattern. For reasons which we do not understand, such an activity of re-enactment heightens the power of the archetype in the lives of the participants, and so releases and directs libidinal energy. In this way the sacrifice of Jesus has achieved those results which we are attempting to describe.

The idea of atonement has often been made the centre of discussions about the achievement of Christ. It is an idea with many aspects, and some of these have only a slight scriptural basis. I shall therefore confine myself to the notion of reconciliation as it is used by Paul.

> God was in Christ, reconciling the world unto himself, not imputing their trespasses unto them (2 Cor. 5. 19).
> For if, when we were enemies, we were reconciled to God by the death of his Son, much more, being reconciled, we shall be saved by his life (Rom. 5. 10).

The presupposition of what Jesus effected is thought of as a state of enmity between God and man. This includes not only man's hostility to God and refusal or failure to do his will, but God's attitude to sinful man, or at least one aspect of it. God, as Jesus taught, loves men and forgives them their sins when they are penitent, and indeed helps them to be penitent; yet at the same time he is stern in his demands, and failure to fulfil these demands is a serious matter, leading to what Paul speaks of as "wrath". From our present standpoint we might perhaps understand "wrath" as the consequences of men's failures, resulting from them in accordance with the laws and principles which, under God, govern the universe. Further, a man's awareness of his failures to fulfil God's demands, and of his inability to make up for these by subsequent good conduct (even if he could be perfectly good), and of his continuing inability to fulfil God's demands, may cause him to despair of attaining to a meaningful life. Such despair may be understood as the result of the appearance of an ego-consciousness; the usual feeling of isolation and weakness here is seen in a context where there is some knowledge of God and of his demands. In these various ways, then, man may be in need of reconciliation.

Reconciliation is effected by Jesus, partly by his teaching about God's love and his readiness to forgive the penitent, and partly by his demonstration of that love in his actions. By living out an archetypal synthesis, Jesus releases libidinal energy in men, which enables them to understand God's nature more fully, to repent and to lead better lives in the future.

Another picture descriptive of the work of Jesus is that of rebirth. He himself spoke to Nicodemus (John 3) about the need for men to be born again. The picture is an appropriate one for the change in a man's life brought about by the release of libidinal energy. It is not necessary here to say more than this, for any attempt to determine the scope of the idea of rebirth would lead us too far away from the main topic.

Largely distinct from the picture of rebirth is that of sonship. John says of Jesus that

> . . . as many as received him, to them gave he power to become the sons of God, even to them that believe on his name: which were born, not of blood, nor of the will of the flesh, nor of the will of man, but of God (John 1. 12 f.).

Paul speaks of Christians becoming sons of God, not through rebirth but through adoption (Gal. 4. 1-7; Rom. 8. 12-17). This idea of sonship includes many aspects of the work of Jesus. It means that men's attitude towards God is one of confidence instead of fear, and that they have a fuller understanding of his purposes. Out of love for the Father, the sons do his will. The adopted sons are "joint-heirs" with Jesus and share in his work. With the exception of the last point, these matters have already been explained sufficiently for present purposes. In regard to the last point, the sharing of the followers of Jesus in his work, we may say that, in so far as the followers manifest in their lives something of the qualities present in Jesus, they are living out aspects of his archetypal synthesis, and this extends its efficacy to people not hitherto touched by it. The martyrs followed Jesus in preferring death to any compromise with the evil powers which opposed them; and thereby the blood of the martyrs became the seed of the Church.

These are by no means all the pictures that have been used to describe and explain the work and achievement of Jesus, but they are among the best-known and most important. What I have tried to show is that there is no fundamental contradiction between them and the modern statement given above, however great the superficial differences. For those who find the traditional accounts foreign to them, most of the points included in the New Testament pictures can be expressed in the terms of the modern statement.

4 THE CONTINUATION OF THE WORK OF JESUS

The achievement of Jesus was to present by his teaching and actions a synthesis of old Testament archetypes capable of bringing about a vast release of libidinal energy. The presentation of the archetypal synthesis was in a sense complete when Jesus died on the cross. What the resurrection and ascension meant to Jesus himself we cannot understand, but we see that in the lives of his followers they mark stages in the advance to domination of the archetypal synthesis. At last, seven weeks after Easter, on the day of Pentecost or Whitsunday, the archetype assumed complete dominance of their lives in a communal experience which they came to describe or interpret as the receiving of the Holy Spirit. With this experience went the great release of libidinal energy. All this naturally had effects which went far beyond the experience itself, especially in two respects. The character of those who had the experience was transformed; and there was a movement of expansion whereby something of the experience came to be shared by large numbers of other men and women.

The transformation of character is in favourable circumstances the normal outcome of a release of libidinal energy. It can be observed in the case of the apostle Peter. Before the crucifixion he was impetuous and hot-headed, and at the same time afraid of the future. After Pentecost he became one of the statesman-like leaders of the growing community, and bold enough to risk his life for the sake of the cause. Characters did not become perfect overnight, of course; human troubles were too deep-rooted for that. Peter himself is accused by Paul of actions which seem to indicate either failure of judgement or moral cowardice (Gal. 2. 14). In the case of Ananias and Sapphira (who pretended to give the entire proceeds of the sale of their property to the Christian community, but held back some) it would seem that there must have been some release of libidinal energy; but the archetypal synthesis of Jesus cannot have become dominant in their lives, since there remained corruption at the centre. This was an exceptional case, however, in a community of several thousands. In general, therefore, it may be said that curative influences were available and operative in individual lives; and in so far as individuals allowed these influences free play in their lives, they were gradually cured of all the troubles which have been described.

The first Christians were those who had witnessed, at least in part, the life, passion, and death of Jesus, that is, his living out of the archetypes. The expansion of the Christian community, that is, its incorporation of other individuals, came about through the preaching of the existing members of the community; and this preaching may be looked on as primarily a presentation of the archetypal synthesis as it was lived out by Jesus. This presentation took place in the context of the life of the Christian community with its transformed characters and its hopeful outlook. This context no doubt facilitated the advance to domination of the archetypal synthesis. Within the community the continued vitality of the archetypal synthesis was ensured by preaching and sacraments. The sacrament of the Eucharist or Holy Communion may be described as an efficacious re-enactment of the important features of the living out by Jesus of the archetypal synthesis. The power or efficacy of the sacrament consists in what may be called its stimulation of the flow of libidinal energy.

The movement of expansion, whereby the outpouring of libidinal energy was widely shared, took place in and through a community. The presentation of the archetypal synthesis was partly by the preaching of the accredited preachers of the community, and partly by the life of the community as a whole. Normally it was only after men and women had been admitted to the community by the rite of baptism that they "received the Holy Spirit". This community had been founded, at least in embryonic form, by Jesus when he appointed twelve men to be with him, for twelve was the number of the tribes of Israel. He originally worked for the acceptance of his teaching by all Israel. When it became clear, however, that most of Israel rejected him, he introduced a new conception. In the distant past Israel had become the people of God through the old testament or covenant, that is, the covenant or treaty-agreement between God and Israel made in the time of Moses. Jesus now spoke of his work, in a figure taken from Jeremiah, as a new testament or covenant to complete, and in some respects supersede, the old. His crucifixion was the sacrifice which instituted the new covenant. The new Israel, the true people of God (since most of the old Israel had turned away from God), were those who accepted him, his teaching, and his archetypal synthesis. They consisted of the Twelve (the place of Judas having been filled by Matthias soon after the resurrection), and those who associated themselves with the Twelve, then or later. This community is the Church, the Israel of God.

In the centuries that have elapsed since then, the Church has been making available to mankind (or at least a portion of it) the healing influences proceeding from the work of Jesus. It has been correcting the inflation of the ego-consciousness and making men humble. It has been bringing them to a truer appreciation of values, curing their neurotic tendencies, and transforming their characters. The opposing influences, however, have been strong, and sometimes the Church has become badly corrupted. It would seem that disunity is usually a sign of corruption somewhere. Nevertheless there has been from time to time a restoration in some measure of the vitality of the archetypal synthesis, and this always led to a fresh release of libidinal energy. At the present time the Church has its failings and its weaknesses, and in general the vitality of its archetypal synthesis appears to be low. Yet the Church of to-day contains areas where its life is comparatively uncorrupt, and where the archetypal synthesis is still alive and even increasing in vitality.

During these centuries there have been releases of libidinal energy outside the Church. There have, for example, been the outpourings connected with the appearance of the world-religion of Islam and, more recently, with the less widely spread religion of Mormonism. Each of these is based on an archetypal synthesis different from the Christian one. Each outpouring occurred on the fringe of Christendom, and one is tempted to suppose that, had the life of the Church been more vigorous, the new movements might have been incorporated within the Church. That did not happen, however; and now the Church, as it faces the problems arising from the unification of the world, finds that it is one of several competitors to provide the archetypal synthesis on which a genuine integration of the world can be based.

It is not for the scholar in his study to pass judgement on the relative merits of the competing religious movements. It is for the adherents of each by word and action to present to the rest of the world the archetypal or symbolic basis of their movement. Victory will rest with the archetypal synthesis which attracts and dominates the great majority of mankind. It is conceivable that this victor may be none of those who at the moment are the obvious competitors; but the likelihood is that the victor will be one of the great world-religions or some modification of it. It is right that man should make efforts to further the cause in which he believes, but he has also to realize that his efforts are puny, and only efficacious when they have the backing of the mighty powers and influences which operate in the unconscious. In the last resort these powers and influences, call them what we may, will determine the future according to their good pleasure.

3

THE CONTEMPORARY APPLICA-
TION OF THE CURE

MANKIND IS not greatly thrilled to learn that nearly two
thousand years ago all human troubles were in essence
cured. What men want is an application of this cure
to the troubles which confront them in their own age. The
present chapter therefore tries to indicate the lines on which
this application may be made. Before dealing with this subject,
however, it is necessary to consider more fully the conception
of archetypes, since these have an important function in the
spread of religion. This consideration of archetypes will also
throw further light on the use of the conception in the previous
chapter.

I THE FUNCTION OF ARCHETYPES IN SOCIETY

The conception of archetypes is derived mainly from the
writings of C. G. Jung, whose pioneer achievement I deeply
admire. To those familiar with his work it will be apparent that
I am greatly indebted to the rich suggestiveness of his thought.
This richness, however, has the incidental disadvantage—if it is
a disadvantage—that it is difficult to give a systematic account of
Jung's views. I shall therefore attempt nothing of this kind.
Instead, I shall give an account of archetypes which is admittedly modelled on what Jung has said, but which does not claim
to be an exact reproduction of his views. Indeed, there will be
some important differences from Jung's views as commonly
understood, since Jung always insists that he does not deal with

metaphysical questions, whereas the present context makes it inevitable to look at archetypes in a wider philosophical setting. Despite these apparent differences, however, the concluding pages of Jung's *Answer to Job,* where he denies that he is an adherent of "psychologism", give me ground for hoping that I have not deviated far from his essential thought.

The nature of archetypes

The conception of archetypes is a postulate of psychology, arising out of psychotherapeutic practice. In view of the autonomy of the special sciences, this conception cannot be questioned by the non-specialist. In so far as the specialists are agreed on accepting it, or even in so far as they are not agreed in rejecting it as worthless, the non-specialist has to accept the conception. What he may do, however, is to examine the evidence on which it is based and suggest a variant interpretation of the evidence which is more in accordance with a comprehensive view of the world.

Archetypes, then, appear as images in the dreams of persons suffering from certain psychical disorders. These images, however, cannot be fully explained from the experience of the persons in question. They appear to rise spontaneously from the unconscious, but they closely resemble images found in mythology, and even in alchemistic writings. Similar images are to be found in the imaginative literature of all ages. Jung has therefore ascribed such images to a "collective unconscious", which somehow or other transcends the individual. Thus the word "archetype" has a twofold meaning. It means both the images and that which produces the images. This latter is a factor within the psyche which sometimes manifests at least a relative autonomy. The autonomy is shown when an individual or a group comes to be possessed by an archetype. In more normal cases the importance of the archetype-factor is not in its autonomy but in the psychical energy which it possesses. Through the images the energies of the psyche are released and are directed to various activities. Intellectual ideas and concepts are probably never effective in directing human life except when, through identification with an archetypal image, they draw on the energy of an archetype-factor.

By way of illustration of an archetype we may take the anima. This occurs only in males, but in females there is the somewhat similar animus. The destructive aspect of this archetype, when it obsesses or possesses a man, is to be seen in the mythological accounts of nixies and female demons. In Rider Haggard's *She* there is a notable literary expression of the figure of the anima. In various primitive forms of religion, such as the religion of the Great Mother, and in Catholic Christian veneration for the Virgin Mary, the anima appears to have a central role. The whole tradition of romantic love, too, is perhaps founded on men's experience of the anima. Thus the anima is projected or manifests itself in various mythological, literary, and religious forms of images. In certain contexts it is convenient to say that these images *are* the archetype; but in other contexts they must be thought of rather as expressions of the archetype, while the archetype is the factor in the psyche which projects or produces these images and responds to them.

This brief account of archetypes is sufficient to show that the conception raises many theoretical problems. To discuss these adequately here would divert us from our main subject. Something must be said, however, about the relation of the archetype to the images in which it expresses itself. The word most frequently used for this is "projection", and it is commonly taken to mean that something internal or subjective is externalized or objectified. The question, then, that it is important to discuss, is whether the image-content of archetypal experiences is essentially internal or subjective.

A common instance of projection is where one criticizes in other people one's own unadmitted faults. Others are in dreams, mythology, and imaginative literature. On the surface, then, there is a strong case for regarding archetype-images as essentially internal or subjective. Rider Haggard's picture of *She* is not the picture of a being in the external physical world, but only the expression of an archetype-factor in his own psyche. Its reality is psychical, but not physical, even though, since the archetype-factor belongs to the collective unconscious, it is shared by all other men.

The superficial view of projection, however, requires modification in two directions. The first is by drawing a distinction between what is merely internal and subjective (as commonly understood) and what is psychically real. As the latter term is used here, a psychical reality is just as much a reality as a physical reality. The second modification is with regard to the relation of archetypal images to external or physical reality. When attention is restricted to dreams and imaginative literature, it is natural to suppose that the images have no relation to external reality. When one extends one's view, however, and considers religious phenomena, it is clear that the archetypal images are related in some way to the external or physical world. The figure of the Great Mother, for example, appears to stand for or signify the vital forces present in the biological functioning of the female. In other words, while it may be true in a sense that the worshippers of the Great Mother have projected psychical contents into the external world, it also appears to be true that they found in the external world something adapted to receiving the projection. In much the same way, when Smith projects his faults on Jones, the faults will sometimes at least be present in Jones.

The heart of the problem appears to be that certain features of the external world evoke in men feelings and responses that are out of proportion to the importance of these features as stimuli. The fact that Jones was stingy does not explain Smith's vehement criticism of his stinginess. The fact that a lady whom the poet saw passing by was sweet and fair does not justify his protestation that he will love her till he die. The same principle may be applied to religious examples, but with limitations. The importance of the vital forces present in woman does not justify, in the eyes of modern man at least, the bloody rites connected with the worship of the Great Mother. On the other hand, the feelings and responses evoked by the great world-religions have made great contributions to the welfare of mankind.

These matters may perhaps be made clearer by bringing them into connection with the conception of religion as the sphere of the meaningful or significant (cf. *The Reality of God*, pp. 103-6). To the worshippers of the Great Mother she presumably stood for or signified the source of what was meaningful in their lives. More particularly this would be the maintenance of life and the production of fresh life. Similarly, the archetypal images at the centre of other religions will be closely linked with what the adherents of each religion regard as meaningful. This is generally some feature of the external world, seen as the setting or basis or source of human life. The archetypal image is not this feature of the external world abstractly conceived, but some concrete embodiment or symbol of it. If one cares to give the name "projection" to the attaching of meaningfulness in this way to a feature of external reality, there is no objection to doing so, provided it is not assumed that meaningfulness is unreal or false, and "projection" is taken only as a convenient name for a process whose nature is to be further investigated.

Even if meaningfulness belongs to psychical reality, there are at least two points where it can be seen to enter into physical reality, namely, in the course of history and in the decisions of an individual. History is full of examples of how men's beliefs about what is meaningful have contributed to determining the course of events. In many decisions, the fact that one course of action would lead to meaningful life, and the alternative course would not do so, is a primary consideration. Thus both a vast historical trend (which is fundamentally a multiplicity of individual or communal decisions) and the decision of a single individual illustrate the basic fact about the human psyche that it responds to the meaningful. Indeed, man cannot escape from responding to the meaningful. When a man attempts to deny that there is anything meaningful, he either lands himself in contradictions or else tacitly and unconsciously adopts some view of what is meaningful. This is an aspect of man's creatureliness.

There are many puzzles here, but we must pass on. It may be noticed, however, that there is a certain appropriateness in linking the conception of meaningfulness with the archetypes. The archetypes are expressed in images which evoke an unexpectedly vigorous response. Meaningfulness is a value, but a value that is superior in grade to other values. Thus there are corresponding features in these two aspects of the same reality. It is also not surprising that the archetypes play a part both in the course of history and in the development of the individual.

The integrative work of archetypes

Because archetypes were discovered in the course of psychiatric practice their destructive or disintegrative effects were clearly seen from the first. The archetype as an autonomous factor may invade and possess the psyche. Yet archetypes also have creative and integrative effects; indeed, they are necessary for the release of psychical energy. Mankind therefore tries to tap this source of energy, but at the same time to avoid its destructive potentialities; we want the vigour of fanaticism without its blindness. To a considerable extent this harnessing of psychical energy to creative purposes has been achieved in the great religions.

The archetypes of the collective unconscious are often described as if they were completely distinct entities and few in number. The trend of recent investigations, however, appears to have been to increase the number, but in so doing to blur the outlines that separate one from another. This is rather what might be expected. It would be strange if the psyche was composed of separate atoms like a chemical compound. The apparent distinctness of the archetypes, then, is not absolute but only relative. That is to say, there are psychical phenomena which are most adequately described in terms of archetypes, but the separate existence of each archetype must not be unduly pressed.

These considerations are relevant to a study of the place of archetypes in the great religions. The great religions are late-comers in human history. When they come upon the scene men already have their primitive religions, and archetypes have a place in these. The precise form or expression of an archetype varies from region to region. At the centre of the great religions —and indeed of every successful religion—there is a complex or system of archetypal forms, which has been referred to else-where in this book as an "archetypal synthesis". Where a new religion appears, the pre-existing religion may be held to have lost its ability to release human energies through its archetypal forms. The archetypal synthesis of the new religion takes the older archetypal forms and transmutes them, and so establishes a new connection with the archetype-factors in the psyche of the people involved. Thus the appearance of a new religion pro-duces an outburst of psychical energy.

These matters have been illustrated in the account of the origin of Christianity given in the previous chapter. The Jewish religion before the mission of Jesus was failing to release and direct the energies of many of its adherents (those whose cir-cumstances made it virtually impossible for them to observe the Law fully), and it was directing the energies of others (the Pharisees) in a wrong direction. This was because its particular archetypal synthesis, and the forms of conduct derived from it, were no longer adequate to the circumstances of the Jews, now that they were incorporated in the Roman empire. Jesus preached and lived out a new archetypal synthesis. In this the elements of the old synthesis were transformed and rearranged; some (like the idea of sacrifice) became more important, others less important. The new synthesis led to a way of life that was more in keeping with contemporary circumstances, in particu-lar with the social contacts between Jews and Gentiles.

It is worth while illustrating this also from the religion of Islam. The dominant religion of Arabia during the early life of

Muhammad was tribal humanism, though there were also vestiges of still earlier religions. With tribal humanism there was associated a system of life that was on the whole adequate to the circumstances of nomads in the desert. This religious and social system, however, was proving unsatisfactory for the settled populations of Mecca and Medina, and indeed was breaking down there. It was to these settled populations that Muhammad addressed his message and it was from them that his most zealous followers came. Symptoms of the breakdown of tribal humanism were a weakening of loyalty to kin and tribe among the stronger men, and a corresponding oppression of the weak by the strong. (A detailed justification of the treatment here will be found in my books, *Muhammad at Mecca* and *Muhammad at Medina*, Oxford, 1953, 1956.)

In the message proclaimed by Muhammad there are three main images or pictures, namely, God, the community, and the messenger; and these are transformations of older archetypal forms and constitute a new archetypal synthesis. The figure of the community of Islam has many features of the Arab tribe, but it had for its basis religion and not real or fictitious blood-kinship. Within the community all men were brothers, and the community, like the tribe, made a high demand on their loyalty. It is not necessary here to investigate further the antecedents of the idea of the community, but the possibility of a close connection with the archetype of the anima may be noted. The second figure is that of the messenger of God. While Europeans commonly speak of Muhammad as a prophet, and the term is indeed frequently used of him by Muslims, his more usual title is that of "the messenger (or apostle) of God"; and this is an indication that Muhammad's function is by no means identical with that of an Old Testament prophet. The figure of the "messenger of God" may be regarded as a transformation of older Arab ideas of the chief of a tribe and likewise of the archaic figures of the old wise man, the king, and the hero. The third figure, that of God, takes up into itself from the Arabian milieu something of the conception of the fate which determines important aspects of man's life. This fate was not an object of worship, however, but was thought of impersonally as "time" or "the days". As judge of all men on the Last Day, God in Islam is the guarantor of the meaningfulness of human life, and in this respect the Islamic idea is a transformation and consummation of notions of deity from the Arab religions prior to tribal humanism.

The archetypal synthesis of Islam is in this way a transformation of archetypal forms which had at some previous period been effective in the lives of the Arabs. To this extent we can understand how the religious movement under Muhammad led to a great release of creative energy. The chief social effect of this religious movement was the unification of Arabia, together with the eradication of older attitudes obstructing that unification. Men were moved deeply enough to be ready to fulfil the demands of the new religion, even when it meant violating all that had hitherto been most sacred, and killing near kinsmen. Because the Islamic community was thus able to evoke men's loyalty and devotion, it was able to achieve a large measure of peace within Arabia, and subsequently within the great empire conquered by the Muslim armies. The blood-feud, which is a primitive and, in certain conditions, an effective way of restricting criminality, was checked and replaced by a more civilized system of justice. While Jews, Christians, and Zoroastrians, regarded as sister monotheistic communities, could have a place as "protected groups" within the Islamic state, pagans and idolaters were considered implacable enemies of Islam. This doctrine of the *jihād* or holy war against polytheists had the social effect of directing outwards the warlike energies of Arab tribes and making it easier to unite them and maintain internal peace.

This brief consideration of the origin of Islam gives some idea of the function of an archetypal synthesis in the formation of a new religious society. Something similar could be said of the unification of the Mediterranean world through the Christianization of the Roman empire, though the process is more complex. Both religions further show how an archetypal synthesis retains much of its effectiveness over a period of centuries. The archetypal synthesis, which is first presented to contemporaries by the preaching and living of the founder of the religion, continues to be presented to wider circles and to fresh generations by the preaching and teaching of adherents of the religion, and by the whole life of the religious community. There may be some slight modifications of the archetypal synthesis in the course of time, but these are usually only changes of emphasis, such as insistence on the virgin birth of Jesus (which was apparently not mentioned by Jesus himself), and comparative neglect of the ceremony of foot-washing. The main features of the archetypal synthesis become stabilized as dogma. The dogmas of a religion are thus the archetypal forms which mediate the release and direction of psychical energy in that religion.

The complex of dogmas of a religion, as the stabilized form of its archetypal synthesis, is to be distinguished from its theology. Theology is the intellectual systematization and elaboration of dogma, and may vary, even in one religion, with the intellectual climate of the particular era and region. A living theology facilitates men's response to the archetypal forms by presenting these forms to them supported by rational considerations. The essential response, however, with its accompanying release of psychical energy, follows directly on the contemplation of the forms. Rational considerations are fruitful in inducing responses where otherwise there would be none, but such responses are generally weaker than those that follow direct contemplation without rational considerations—in much the same way as a man's romantic love for a girl is stronger if he has not thought about reasons for loving her.

Despite this distinction in principle between dogma and theological doctrine, it is often difficult in practice to separate the two. The Christian dogma of the atonement, for example, can hardly be stated fully without implying some theological doctrine of the atonement. As a consequence it sometimes happens, especially where there has been a change of intellectual climate, that a dogma becomes discredited because the theological elaboration of it passes out of fashion. The remedy for this loss of the power to release psychical energy is a return to the dogma in its pure form, that is, to the original experiences on which the religion is based.

A religious cult, that is, acts of worship, may be regarded as a presentation of archetypal forms, together with at least a token response on the part of the worshippers. In Islam the Worship, or formal prayers, having as climax the prostration of the worshippers, foreheads touching the ground, is an acknowledgement of God's omnipotence and man's creatureliness. The Christian sacrament of baptism is a presentation of the power of God to "wash away" sin; the candidate for baptism, either himself or through sponsors (godparents), acknowledges his actual sin and his implication in a sinful world order, and by a symbolic act of washing is freed from the entail of the past. The Christian eucharist is a presentation of the sacrificial death of Christ, and, by communicating, Christians participate in the benefits of the sacrifice. The effect of these solemn presentations of archetypal forms is to maintain, and even increase, the response to them and the concomitant release of psychical energy.

In the great religions the systematization of the original archetypal synthesis through the elaboration and development of theology, worship, and general organization has been on the whole beneficial. The activity of the archetypal factors in the psyche has been canalized and directed towards socially useful ends. In this way the individual has been largely protected from the dangers that often accompany the activity of archetypes. At the same time, because the canalizing of psychical energy involves some restraint, there may be a certain loss of energy and of spontaneity.

The great world religions have become what they are, not because of the violence with which psychical energy was released in the experience of their founders, but because of their success in directing energy into channels that were socially fruitful and beneficial. Many men have probably had religious experiences as deep as those of the great religious leaders. The reason that millions have come to share the experience of the leaders is that, in an age of maladjustment, the new social attitudes linked with the leaders' experience made it possible for men to readjust themselves to circumstances. Where large numbers of men respond to the same archetypal synthesis, and where their responses are directed into socially fruitful channels, there is a large measure of social unification and integration. To revert to what was said about integration in *The Reality of God*, archetypal factors and archetypal synthesis may be regarded as instruments through which the principle of integration in any society operates.

2 THE PRINCIPLES OF APPLYING THE CURE

The position now reached in the argument is this. It has been shown that Jesus effected a cure in essence for all human troubles, and that he did this by proclaiming and living out an archetypal synthesis. Mankind has still many troubles, however, because the cure has not been applied to all human life. For one thing, not all human beings accept the Christian archetypal synthesis. For another thing, in the lives of many who professedly accept it, the synthesis has ceased to evoke much response. In many cases, too, even those who respond are not sure about the attitudes to adopt in the new circumstances in which they find themselves. These matters are involved in considering how to apply the cure.

In using the phrase "applying the cure", there is a caution to be observed. The phrase suggests that what we have in view is primarily a piece of human planning, of much the same character as designing a new type of aircraft. Now we can certainly plan to some extent for an application of the cure, but only to some extent. Ultimately it is not we who control the archetypal factors; on the contrary we are controlled by them, and by the hierarchy of principles of integration working through them. We cannot by planning, no matter how thorough, reach the archetypal form which will evoke a dynamic response from slumbering factors in the psyche of thousands and millions of men. Only the religious genius can produce the archetypal synthesis at the basis of widespread movements, and he does not reach it by planning or intellectual processes; rather it is thrust upon him by the archetypal factors in his psyche. At most we can plan for repetitive presentations of archetypal forms, which have first been creatively presented by the religious genius, but we cannot predict the response. Planning, or the control of human life by intellect, is thus subordinate to great movements of the human spirit lying beyond its control. Talk about applying the cure belongs to the sphere of intellect, and we must therefore keep in mind the limits to what intellect can achieve.

In a similar way we must avoid an undue pride in what Christianity can achieve, and an overestimate of its present strength. Even if Jesus effected in essence the cure of all human troubles, yet the Christians of to-day are far from having the specific answer to every contemporary problem. There is a sense in which, during the last four hundred years or so, Christians have moved further away from the growing-point of human life, that is, the point at which contemporary troubles are being met and tackled. Not merely has leadership in the intellectual field passed to scientists and scientifically-minded philosophers. Even in the moral field in which Christians claim leadership, the running has been made of late by Marxists, for it is they who have made people aware of the evils of exploitation and of the class struggle. We Christians, despite the glorious message we have in the Gospel, must be very humble when we prescribe remedies for the troubles of to-day. We have the cure in essence, but we have not worked it out very far in detail; in some cases we are not even in the positions from which problems can be tackled, since only those who are so immersed in some area of life that they know in detail the nature of its problems are in a position to begin tackling them. With this limitation also, then, in mind, let us proceed.

The fundamental contribution of Christianity to the alleviation of the troubles of to-day is an archetypal synthesis capable of evoking a response sufficiently strong to correct false tendencies in man's psyche. So far, however, only about a quarter of mankind, perhaps less, accept the Christian synthesis, and, despite great missionary efforts, this number is not increasing rapidly. The path from acceptance of the Christian synthesis to the removal of our troubles is not an easy one, but, even if it were easy, it would not be open to the non-Christian three-quarters of mankind. The bringing of these hundreds of millions to accept the Christian synthesis is thus a task with high priority. Unfortunately the Christian missionary effort suffers from the weakness of the Christian archetypal synthesis in the lives of Christians. It is seldom possible for a daughter church or community to have a deeper and stronger religious life than its mother. In so far as the archetypal synthesis has lost its power to evoke a vigorous response among those who consider themselves Christians, it cannot be much more effective in a group of recent converts. Other factors have certainly contributed to the slow progress of the Christian mission, such as its foreignness to most Asian and African peoples, and its excessive individualism. There is also the mysterious fact that, however well a religious message is presented, some men reject it, just as many of Jesus' contemporaries rejected him. When every allowance is made for these considerations, however, much of the responsibility for the slow advance must be assigned to the weakness at the heart of Christendom. This weakness must therefore be looked at.

One symptom—perhaps the most important symptom—of the weakness of Christians' response to the archetypal synthesis is our failure to bring the whole of our conduct into relation with our Christian dogma. There are great areas of life where our activity, and the thinking on which it is based, has nothing specifically Christian in it. Examples of this will be given later in this chapter. It is not merely in trivial matters or technical matters that this happens, but in matters which have a central place in the life of human society. At the growing-point of human life Christians are largely absent, and their place has been taken by adherents of other dogmas, such as humanists and Marxists. Thus Christians have lost the initiative in many fields, and in dealing with the great contemporary problems men are turning to humanism and Marxism for guidance and not to Christianity. While this trend has only become noticeable within the last century or so, it may be traced back at least to the strong current which entered European life at the Renaissance. From that time onward there was a growing reliance on man and his intellect. Many thinkers who professed Christianity were almost entirely uninfluenced by it in their thinking. So the trend grew, until we all speak and think about solving problems, that is, about relying on intellect to overcome our difficulties. The present confusion in the higher parts of the sphere of intellect has not lessened our trust in it appreciably, though the strength of Christian dogma has been reduced by a lack of intellectual understanding of the function of dogma, and through the association of dogma with outmoded philosophy.

When all this has been said, and much more has been thought, how can we set about planning for the application of the Christian cure to the troubles of our contemporary world? In a sense we are planning for a unitary world-order, indeed for a Christian world-order; but what the Christians can give men is not the blue-print of such an order, but instructions about how to conduct themselves in their present circumstances in the immediate future. The greatest of journeys begins with a single step, and it must be taken from where a man is already standing. These instructions may be arranged under three heads.

1. We must try to deepen our appreciation of the archetypal synthesis and our response to it. Since such matters are beyond our control, we have no infallible way of doing this; but it has been observed that a deeper response to archetypal forms often follows prolonged contemplation of them. That is to say, we

must contemplate the fundamental forms of the Christian synthesis as they are recorded in the gospels, and as they are re-
petitively presented in Christian worship. From such contemplation there is a chance that we shall receive deeper insight and
more dynamic energy.

2. We must try to apply the new attitudes derived from this
contemplation to the spheres of daily living in which we are
immersed. In so far as a man has a concern for affairs in these
spheres, he will receive insight about them in the course of contemplation, and this will lead to the application. In most cases,
however, intellect will play a large role. This comes about in
two ways. Firstly, men can learn from observing how forms of
conduct and social organization work out in practice. Indeed
some basis of experience of this kind is essential in all social and
moral reform (cf. *The Reality of God*, p. 85). Further, the
knowledge gained from experience in this field is not peculiar
to Christians but is shared by all men of practical wisdom; many
Christians have far less of this knowledge than the wise
humanist. Thus many of the statements to be made later in this
chapter are put forward as matters of common observation,
which are only to be accepted in so far as they agree with the
observation of others.

Secondly, however, there are some points where the Christian
outlook gives a sounder understanding of what is happening in
society, and of the lines on which reform is immediately possible. Since Christianity teaches that inflation of the self is at
the root of all our troubles, the Christian observing social affairs
will make a careful search for traces of inflation both in individuals and in groups, and will be likely to discover important
points that might easily escape the non-Christians. Again, the
Christian ought to be more aware than the non-Christian that
man is imperfect, and that man's selfishness and other imperfections render impracticable Utopian solutions of problems
that presuppose a high degree of unselfishness. At the same
time the Christian will avoid the opposite error of taking too
low a view of human nature, since he will realize that, though

man is imperfect, he is capable of overcoming at least some of his imperfection, and that therefore, in favourable conditions, a society may gradually achieve a higher general level of morality; in this way solutions of problems may become practicable which were formerly impracticable. These are essentially matters of observation on which the non-Christian might be expected to agree with the Christian, but in practice they are often disregarded by humanists, and even by Christians infected by humanism. The close connection, however, of these matters with Christian dogma makes it more likely that the Christian will be aware of them.

3. We must try to extend the application of the cure to all spheres of life. One kind of extension is to attempt to bring more people to accept the Christian archetypal synthesis and to respond to it. This is, of course, what is commonly understood by evangelism, or missionary work. Another kind of extension is to try to apply the Christian cure to aspects of life to which it has not yet been applied—an activity sometimes described as that of "the frontier". Success in thus extending the application of the cure does not necessarily follow on even the most careful planning, since such matters are partly beyond human control. What a man may deliberately do is to immerse himself in the life of a non-Christian society, or in an un-Christianized sector of the life of his own society, but what happens after that depends on the working of the archetypal factors in his psyche and the psyche of those with whom he is in contact.

In all attempts to "apply the cure" to various spheres there would seem to be more chance of success if the practical measures to be taken are in close organic connection with the archetypal synthesis. It is not easy to define precisely what is meant by "close organic connection". Perhaps an example will suffice. At first glance there seems to be no connection between the central dogmas of Islam and the permission to marry four wives, which might be due to a temporary excess of women. On examination, however, it proves that the system of allowing a man to have four wives was introduced in order to stop the oppression and exploitation of female wards by unscrupulous guardians. Further, such oppression was one symptom of the breakdown of traditional morality through the growth of individualism; and this breakdown was dealt with by the dogma that God judges men on the Last Day, since this dogma provides a sanction for a new individualistic morality. Thus the system of marriage is closely connected with a central concern of the religion of Islam.

In the remaining sections of this chapter an attempt is made to establish links between the archetypal synthesis of Christianity and measures to deal with general problems of our time, in which, whether we realize it or not, we are all immersed.

3 THE APPLICATION TO PARTICULAR SOCIETIES

An analysis of the present malaise

One of the great problems of our time is the malaise and dissension within particular societies, that is, roughly speaking, within nations. The most obvious symptom of this trouble is class hatred, but there are also others. A consideration, however, of class hatred, and what is involved in it, and what has led up to it, will show sufficient of the total problem to serve as basis for a profitable discussion of how the Christian is to deal with it.

A body politic such as Great Britain, is, in one sense, already a unity, although in another sense there may be varying degrees of unity in a body politic of this kind. Unity in this second sense might also be described as harmony or integration. The present lack of harmony in Great Britain, as in many other countries, may be traced chiefly to the Industrial Revolution. This is not to say that there was complete harmony in Britain before then, for there certainly were disharmonies. The most obvious of our present disharmonies, however, are due to the Industrial Revolution, since that led to the break-up of a comparatively stable order of society. In the series changes that constitute that revolution the strong exploited the weak. The strong may not have realized that their conduct was bad, for in the new circumstances of the time there were no accepted principles of conduct to guide them. Seen from the standpoint of the present day, however, much of what they did was exploitation and was bad.

In the course of time the weak realized their common interest in resisting their exploitation by the strong. They banded themselves together in trade unions, and later also in the Labour Party. The trade unions discovered that, if the weak, the employees, joined in withholding their labour from the strong, the employers, they could wrest from them some amelioration of wages and other conditions. As the country became more industrialized, and as the labour movement in its various aspects became better organized, the strength of the latter increased until under the Labour government of 1945-51 certain key industries were nationalized, that is, taken from the strong of former days, the employers, and placed under national control. This is how matters stand at the moment.

In this whole process certain religious issues are implicit. From the standpoint of this book, with its insistence that the appearance of self-consciousness is at the root of our troubles, these religious issues can conveniently be studied by directing attention to the ideas of security, equality, and freedom.

A feeling of insecurity is one of the results of the appearance of self-consciousness in groups and individuals. When groups or individuals become conscious of themselves as distinct from others, they lose something of the sense of belonging together in a greater unity and of being supported by this unity. When things go well with a group it tends to magnify its success unduly. When things go badly with a group, it seeks alliances with other groups, that is, it tries to merge itself in a greater whole. One of the functions of bodies politic, of whatever size, is to provide their members with security. This includes security for life and property from both external enemies and internal criminals, and also a measure of fair play in dealings between members of the body politic. Where there is a change in the social order such as there was during the Industrial Revolution, practices which were not condemned under the old order come to be regarded as unfair by those who suffer from them. To this extent these people come to feel insecure, and begin a search for security.

The trade union movement, whose growth is one of the remarkable features of the last century, is essentially a series of alliances between individuals and groups who had come to feel insecure. They found that they were bound together by a common need to resist exploitation and by a common desire for certain kinds of security. In this century of trade union growth and in relation to it, a subdivision of society, the class, has come to have a prominence that did not belong to it previously. There always have been social classes, of course, but there is probably no parallel elsewhere to the consciousnes of solidarity that has been attained in the working class. This consciousness of solidarity is found chiefly among employees of industrial concerns, and only to a lesser extent among farm-labourers, smallholders, and peasants. Though we sometimes speak about "a middle class" as a single entity, it has no comparable sense of solidarity, and, as often as not, we use a plural and speak about "the middle classes". Similarly, there is no sense of class solidarity among employers, even though the strength of the trade unions, among other factors, has forced them to seek security by forming associations. Still less is there any solidarity among the policy-holders of an insurance company, though these are in a sense combining with one another in the search for security. In the light of these contrasts the achievement of working-class solidarity is all the more remarkable. Indeed, it brings to the fore a new potential basis for social unification or integration, namely, economic function.

Every group that feels insecure exaggerates its own merits and decries those of its rivals, and the trade union movement, growing out of the search for security, is no exception to this rule. This may be seen in the tendency to magnify the importance of the kinds of work done by members of trade unions, and to overlook or deny the importance of other economic functions, such as those of employers and financiers, or to criticize adversely the way in which these functions are performed in the present social and economic system.

While a measure of security has thus been found by combining with other individuals and groups, and by realizing the solidarity of the working class, there has gone along with this a reliance on another source of security, namely, money and property. To rely on wealth in some form or other is one of the deepest-rooted tendencies in human nature, and is, if anything, more prevalent among the rich than among the poor, as Jesus was constantly saying. We are all to some extent like the rich man in one of the gospel stories (Luke 12. 16-21). He was a land-owner, and had had several bumper harvests; and he thought that, if he built larger barns, and stored the surplus, he would have full security against bad harvests for a number of years—not realizing that his death was imminent. In pressing for higher wages, then, the trades unions have been acting on the basis of an omnipresent human attitude, and no criticism can be made of their policy that would not be relevant to nearly all the human race. Nevertheless, it is important from our present standpoint to realize the extent to which reliance on wealth to give security is a basis of trade union activity. Once the trade union movement became well established, pressure for higher wages was merged in a struggle with the employers over the division of the proceeds of industry and also over control of the capital. This leads, however, to a discussion of the idea of equality. As time went on, experience showed that high wages gave no security unless a man was certain of getting work. Thus a wider conception of social security became popular, which included not merely unemployment insurance but also services, such as the health service, provided either without payment, or at a nominal cost.

While the welfare state as we now have it in Britain is thus in part the outcome of the working-class demand for security and equality, it also proceeds to some extent from earlier ideas, according to which all members of a body politic or political society were brothers, so that it was the concern of the society as a whole, and especially of those who exercised administrative functions in it, that no member of it should be without the bare necessities of existence. What the working-class demands have brought about is the general acceptance of a much more generous interpretation of the minimal standard of living.

The idea of equality has a sufficiently prominent place in the present social unrest to deserve separate consideration, although it would appear to be derivative from the idea of security. In an age of social change, when men see some of their fellows rising in wealth and position, and others falling, their awareness of their separate individuality and consequent insecurity makes them demand equality. There are, of course, many kinds of equality. To name only a few there are equality before the law, equality of reward, and equality of educational opportunity. Inequality usually means unfairness; and if a man is afraid of unfair treatment, say in the law courts, he feels insecure.

It is impossible, of course, to have absolute equality. Men differ in natural abilities and in character. They differ in age. As diversion of labour increases with the growth of industrialization, men increasingly differ in function. In a comparatively stable society, however, allowance is made for these inevitable differences. Certain differentials (as they are now being called) in reward are held to be right and proper, and, so long as the recognized scheme of differences is adhered to, a man does not feel that he is unjustly treated when his wage is less than another man's. When social change begins, however, inequalities tend to be felt as unfair, and the demand for equality is widespread, until a new set of differentials comes to be generally accepted. In Britain at the present time the demand for equality in earnings, and equality in wealth, has probably been given a fuller practical expression than it has ever had previously in civilized society. There is greater equality in Britain than in the U.S.S.R. The need for differentials, however, is now coming to be realized, and the equalitarian tide has perhaps begun to ebb.

Although the demand for equality arises out of the desire for security, equality in practice may lead to some insecurity. This may be discerned in some of the recent disputes about differentials between skilled and responsible workers, like engine-drivers, and less skilled workers. Even within the working class there is a tendency to look down on the lowest-paid, unskilled workers. A reduction of the difference between the skilled worker and the unskilled worker is not merely financially disadvantageous to the skilled worker and felt by him to be unfair; it is also a reduction of his social status and of his significance in the life of the country, and this, probably more than the pecuniary side of the matter, fosters a sense of insecurity.

The idea of freedom is mainly a negative one. The closely related idea of self-determination is more positive, but it also has an important negative side. In a society where economic changes have made social changes necessary, freedom is of great value to enable men to make the necessary readjustments. This includes freedom from authority and from tradition in various forms. Individuals and groups become aware of limitations, restrictions, and hindrances, and begin to demand freedom, where some features of the social system are no longer appropriate to existing conditions and need adjustment. As the society moves towards a new stability there are fewer features of the system which give rise to frustration, and consequently less demand for freedom. While in a transitional society the demand for freedom is justified, it is not without its dangers. A rapid dissolution of those sectors of the old social order where adjustment is required may cause a widespread feeling of insecurity which is worse than the evils to be remedied. Thus, in a changing society, there is an inevitable opposition between those who want to hasten the granting of freedom and those who want to slow it down.

The Christian attitude in general

After the above consideration of some of the religious issues involved in the internal troubles of the various countries of the world, and of Britain in particular, the question has to be faced, What is the Christian attitude in these matters? It seems best to speak about an "attitude", for the primary Christian concern is not with possible political programmes or economic measures but with the corruption in men's hearts. Moreover, what is said ought to be acceptable to all Christians, and such agreement belongs to the level of attitude rather than to the level of practical measures. At the latter level there is often room for legitimate disagreement between Christians. In general—though exceptions may sometimes be justified—the Christian does not because of his Christian allegiance cease to be a member of the various groups to which he naturally belongs, such as his nation, his social class, his local community, and his family; and loyalties to these groups have a part in determining the practical measures he takes or supports. Since most Christians are followers and not leaders, their public activities consist in supporting measures initiated by others, and not in themselves initiating measures.

Further, the Christian attitude with regard to the internal affairs of Britain should be connected with Christian dogma. What has just been said about a man acting in accordance with his group membership links up with the Christian dogma of the incarnation. Just as God took human form and thus became immersed in human life, so the man in whom the Divine (as the Holy Spirit) is operative deliberately wills, in normal cases, that he should remain immersed in the life of the groups in which he finds himself. The most important connection with Christian dogma, however, is in respect of the insecurity and inflation of the self that appeared as self-consciousness emerged. The above analysis has shown that security and insecurity are all-pervasive elements in the present situation. The dominant concern of Christians is a restoration of the wholeness that was lost in achieving self-consciousness, or perhaps rather we should say that their concern is the advance to a new self-conscious wholeness which will replace the original wholeness that was lost.

The wholeness of society at which the Christian aims is one

where the members of the society are fully aware that they belong together and form a partnership for the business of living. A large part of the purpose of any society is simply to maintain itself in life. This is the conscious acceptance of the urge of the life in us to multiply itself. The maintenance of life, however, is not the entire aim of the higher societies. They also try, in the course of maintaining themselves biologically, to exemplify high and noble qualities of life. One might say that the urge of life was to expand not merely quantitatively, but qualitatively. For the maintenance of life, it is of course necessary for a society to have a satisfactory material and economic basis; but a high degree of wholeness or integration is also needed, and this is more particularly the concern of Christians, though it cannot be entirely separated from the material aspects.

The story from the gospels already referred to, about the farmer who built larger barns and thought he was secure for several years, only to discover that his death was imminent, is a constant reminder to Christians that material security is never more than relative. At the same time, great importance is attached, both in the gospels and in the rest of the New Testament, to the social system, especially in its political aspects, as a source of security. In short, social security in a very wide sense has always been a concern of Christians, even though they were aware of its relative character. After these preliminaries, let us turn to our own society.

One of the features of the last century has been the appearance of a new principle of social integration. A new social class (or classes) has grown into consciousness of itself, and the basis of its unity is what may be called for short the common economic function of its members. More precisely, it is the common status of the members as employees in the organization of industry, commerce, and agriculture. However we describe the basis, a large measure of unification has been achieved, and for those concerned with wholeness the question arises whether this principle may become the basis of the unification of an entire society. The working-class movement itself believes that such a unification is possible, and expresses this belief in the conception of the "classless society".

One of the difficulties in the extension of working-class unity to the whole of society is that the middle classes have hitherto felt themselves to be superior to the class represented by the trade union movement. In this way, about half the members of our society would seem to be excluded by their own attitude from the new unity. This difficulty, however, is perhaps not so serious as it seems to be. One alleviation comes from the very success of the trade union movement, which has placed skilled artisans in a higher wage-group than many "white-collar" men. An increase in wages does not, of course, lead immediately to the adoption of those attitudes associated with the middle classes; but there is a fair chance that in time it will do so, if the relative improvement in wages is maintained. Another alleviation is that, in the professions, unions analogous to the trade unions are becoming important, while professional men are increasingly moving from the status of "self-employed" to that of "employee"—doctors and dentists, for example. Thus the working class, and at least the lower middle classes, are tending to merge into one another, and there are grounds for hoping that the distinction between the classes would not be a hindrance to a greater integration of society. Perhaps before long we shall see a common council for trade unions and professional unions.

The most serious aspect of the difficulty is psychological, namely, the attitude of the middle classes, and also to some extent that of the working class. The latter will be more conveniently discussed at a later stage in the argument. Meanwhile let us consider the middle classes' feeling of superiority. This feeling appears to be bound up with the belief that intellectual work is superior to manual work, and such a belief may be supported by the fact that man's superiority to the animals depends on his intellect. Our whole educational system tends to foster this belief, since a large part of its function is to discover intellectual ability and train it. There is another element, however, in the feeling of middle class superiority. The middle classes feel that their contribution to the life of the community is an important one. The emphasis is on the importance of what they do, and because they suffer from the universal human weakness, they tend to exaggerate this importance, and the exaggeration takes the form of asserting that the kinds of work done by the middle classes are more important than the kinds of work done by the working class.

This discussion of the relative importance of intellectual and manual work may seem trivial, yet questions of great moment are involved. It is a universal demand, though it may be expressed in different ways, that a man's life should be meaningful or significant; and normally this is not so unless the man is performing a meaningful function in society. Because human beings are imperfect, however, and have a lurking sense of insecurity, they are not content just to know that their function in the life of society is meaningful. They also want to believe that their function is important, and, indeed, more important than the functions of other people. Thus the exaggerated views of the importance of intellectual work spring from an attempt to assert that intellectual workers have a meaningful function in the life of society, even though some people think that "they are not really doing anything".

The very use of the term "working class" is mixed up with these questions. In part it derives from exaggerating the importance of manual work, as if it was the only real work. There is also another side. The word "work" has been used so far in this discussion with the connotation of "the performance of some operation which is useful for society or some part of society". It may have another connotation, however, namely, "what is unpleasant, undesirable and irksome about the performance of such operations"—in short, the drudgery of work. When work is thought of in this way, then it becomes something to be avoided as far as possible. In a society which thinks in this way there comes to be a division between the "workers" who perform the more irksome kinds of work, and the élite who are able to avoid these kinds of work. Thus "worker" comes to have a depreciatory sense.

The existence of differences between the working class and the middle classes is thus a serious difficulty for the extension of working-class unity to the whole of society—that is, for the growth of a "classless society"—but it is not insurmountable. The root of the matter is in men's attitude to their work and to their fellow-workers. The Christian position which is the basis of a new attitude might be stated as follows. A human society naturally tries to maintain itself in being, and for this purpose the members of the society have to perform many operations and engage in many activities. In most of these operations and activities there is felt to be something irksome. This feeling of irksomeness is due to the appearance of self-consciousness in groups and individuals, and to the consequent loss of the sense of oneness with the rest of mankind and, more generally, with the rest of the universe. The feeling should grow less as the sense of oneness is recovered. While our sense of oneness remains imperfect, however, we have to accept the fact that, as individuals and as a society, we must perform irksome tasks in order to keep ourselves alive. It has been found by experience that the tasks are most efficiently performed when men specialize in particular jobs. Because of this there is in the modern world a very high degree of specialization and of division of labour, so that a man comes to spend his life in one type of activity, whether it is farming, type-setting, or driving railway engines. In so far as these activities all contribute to the good life of society, they are all equally meaningful. The national society, like the Christian community (cf. 1 Cor. 12), is analogous to a living body; and, just as the various parts and organs of the body are all necessary to the functioning of the body, and cannot be placed in order of merit, so the various types of work cannot be placed in order of merit. Fundamentally, the work of the dustman is just as meaningful as that of the Prime Minister. Both contribute to the good life of society.

In actual societies there is a minority of individuals who keep themselves alive by activities that are socially undesirable. In this class would come burglars and prostitutes. Other activities are on the border-line between contributing and not contributing to the good of society, for example, promoting football pools. An activity such as this might be defended by saying that in the present condition of society it provides men with some entertainment, and that, if there were no football pools, there might be something worse. If the question whether football pools are desirable or undesirable is left aside, it may be generally admitted that wholesome entertainment is a genuine contribution to the good life of society. Another case which might cause hesitation is that of the private capitalist, and this will be discussed presently. Meanwhile, if it is agreed that most activities contribute to the good life, and in so far as they do so are equally meaningful, then there is no reason why any one kind of worker should look down on any other kind of worker; that is to say, there is no reason for any class hatred of the sort that exists at present. In this sense the Christian is bound to accept the idea of a classless society. Moreover, the Christian contributes to the realization of the classless society when he insists on the dignity of all socially desirable work, and on the fundamental unity of all who contribute to the good life of their society.

A second difficulty in the extension of working-class unity to the whole of society is that this unity has a negative aspect. The working class discovered its unity because employees needed to band themselves together to resist exploitation by employers. That is to say, the aim was not so much the positive one of creating something good as the negative one of removing something bad. This element of negativity has two consequences. In so far as exploitation is checked or stopped—and in Britain the working-class movement has had a large measure of success— the *raison d'être* of the unity disappears; while the fundamental place in the working-class movement of antagonism to employers would seem to make it impossible to extend the unity of the movement in such a way as to include employers.

In comment on these two points it may be admitted that, in

Britain at least, divergences of interest between different trade unions have begun to appear. In the course of time these divergences might destroy the unity of the working class, if it is conceived merely as an association of groups with like material interests with a view to securing these interests. This is not the whole truth, however. Even if the working-class movement started from common material interests, in the course of its growth a more fundamental basis for unity has become discernible, namely, economic function. This is something that has probably been present all along, though men are not even yet fully aware of it. Yet the fact that men share in certain functions in the economic process (which is the life of society in its material or economic aspect) does draw them together. In so far as working-class unity is conceived as having a basis of this sort there is hope that it may be extended to the whole of society —provided all the members of the society are performing economic functions which contribute to the good life of the society. This way of looking at the matter provides a positive basis for unity, which ought to survive the attainment of the negative aims of the working-class movement. Does it make it possible for employers to be included in what we have called "the extension of working-class unity", Or can the classless society be attained only through the "liquidation" of all employers?

It would be admitted by members of the working class that a useful function in the economic process is performed by employers, that is, by private capitalists or *entrepreneurs* who start factories and other undertakings in which men are employed. The objection to private capitalism is not that it performs no economic function, but that in its performance of its function there are serious disadvantages, whereas the same functions can be performed in other ways that do not have socially undesirable consequences. The disadvantages of private capitalism are mainly two: it gives too great power, economic and political, to individuals; and it gives an undue share of the profit of an enterprise to the employer.

The first charge against private capitalism is true. The whole trend of industrialization is towards larger and larger companies and combines, with ever-increasing "rationalization" and co-ordination. This inevitably places great power in the hands of a few individuals. It is a primary interest of society that this power should not be used irresponsibly to secure private advantages without regard to what would be beneficial for the society as a whole. Most industrialized countries have therefore adopted various devices to reduce the power of private individuals or to ensure that it is used responsibly. In some cases industries have been nationalized; in others legislation has been made restricting the activities of companies in various ways. Some of the chief abuses of power have thus been made impossible, but the problem is still very far from being solved. It is essentially a problem of power and of ensuring that power is wielded for the good of society as a whole. The growth of technology in the last century and a half has made great concentrations of power inescapable. If it is not in the hands of a private capitalist, it will be in the hands of a civil servant or a politician; and it is not to be assumed that either of the latter two is *bound* to wield the power more wisely than the private capitalist.

It is important to emphasize the complexity of the problem. The nature of the power is different in the transport, steel, and newspaper industries respectively, and the probability is therefore that different methods of control are necessary. Again, a method that successfully controlled an industry in one European country might be unsatisfactory in another European country and totally inadequate in an Asiatic or African country. A measure of experiment is thus necessary, though each country should be ready to learn what it can from the experiments of other countries. The Christian has no special faculty which enables him to predict the results of such experiments. His aim in this sphere should be to see that power is wielded for the good of society, and in such a way as to promote a greater degree of unity and harmony both in the national society and in the society of mankind as a whole.

The second charge against private capitalism is partly true, in that some *entrepreneurs* derive from their enterprise a share of the product which, compared with that of the employees, is enormous. This raises the question of equality of reward, which is to be discussed presently. Meanwhile, let us anticipate the result of that discussion, namely, that under present circumstances, and in the foreseeable future, some inequalities in men's reward for their work is not merely inevitable but justifiable; and let us see whether this justifies the high rewards gained by some *entrepreneurs*.

The alternative system to that of private capitalism is state enterprise, that is, the administration of an undertaking by public officials controlled directly or indirectly by the state. The drawback of this system is that it is liable to be inefficient. There are, of course, some state enterprises which show a high degree of efficiency. It will usually be found, however, that these efficient state enterprises operate, like the post office, in monopoly conditions, where the risks are comparatively small. In most industrial enterprises, on the other hand, there is a large amount of risk, and it is difficult for the public official, because of his relation to society, to make balanced decisions on questions involving risk. On the one hand, if his whole career and livelihood depend on his position as an official, his chief concern will be to show himself reliable, and he will therefore avoid setting on foot risky undertakings. This is the mentality often found in a civil service. On the other hand, if a man holds a responsible public position, but is not wholly dependent for his livelihood on it, he may be inclined to take undue risks with public money. The reason is that, if the enterprise succeeds, it will be greatly to his credit, whereas, if it does not succeed, he will not suffer greatly in reputation or any other way. The ground-nut fiasco of the late 1940s is an outstanding example of this.

The moral is that in matters involving risk men are most likely to decide wisely, and to attain the golden mean between timidity and rashness, where they stand to gain largely if the enterprise succeeds, but to lose largely if it fails. That is to say, private capitalism performs useful functions for society as a whole at least in certain types of industrial enterprise; and these functions cannot be so well performed in any other way. This is particularly so in Britain, where there is a long tradition of industrial and commercial enterprise. It would therefore seem that in enterprise of a pioneering character, or where risk is involved, it is better for society as a whole to retain capitalism, but to try to limit the power and wealth that success places in the hands of individuals. This would appear to be a matter where each country must proceed by careful experiment. The Christian attitude should be that the private *entrepreneur* is worthy of respect in so far as he is making a useful contribution to the life of society, and in so far as his reward is not out of proportion to the importance of his contribution.

The Christian attitude to equalitarianism

The last remark is a reminder that the question of equality of reward has yet to be considered. The Christian holds that all men are essentially equal. All have been created by God, all are involved in the corruption which has resulted from the appearance of self-consciousness, all are capable of benefiting from the cure achieved by Jesus, and all are to be judged by God on the Last Day. For the Christian what ultimately matters is the judgement of God, and it is made without respect for social status. Kings and aristocrats may be punished and humble labourers rewarded. From this fundamental equality, however, it cannot be deduced that other kinds of equality are desirable in the present state of the world. If men were perfect, equality of reward would doubtless be the rule, except in so far as men vied with one another to make do with less than their fair share. Unfortunately men are imperfect, and try to find security through having a little more than their fair share. In the future men may become less selfish, but at the moment we must base our plans on the assumption of a large measure of selfishness.

Inequality of reward appears to be due to three types of causes: to the scarcity of certain intellectual and other talents, and their consequent high market value; to various historical accidents and illogicalities; and to a widespread desire to feel important, and to have this importance marked by a superior social status and higher rewards. Let us deal with these in order.

1. The scarcity of men and women of outstanding ability in various fields should be a commonplace, though it is sometimes questioned. Where there are many candidates for highly paid jobs, however, it does not follow that the salary might be reduced. There may be no one with proper qualifications among the applicants, since all properly qualified persons may already have better jobs. This, indeed, appears to be what is happening in Britain in many spheres. In such a situation, then, where talent is scarce and men are imperfect, differentials in respect of monetary reward seem to be the best way of distributing the abilities of the nation where they are most needed. If an attempt was made to give the same wage to everyone, there would be a rush for some jobs and a rush to avoid others. According to their temperament men would look for jobs where the work was easy or the conditions pleasant, or where they had power over other people, and avoid those where the work was unpleasant or difficult. If only incompetent persons were available for important and responsible positions, the affairs of the country as a whole would soon be in a great muddle. To attempt to dictate to men the jobs they were to do would not help greatly, since unwilling workers are nearly always inefficient. The system of differential rewards in a more or less free market leads to a tolerably efficient distribution of abilities. At the moment there does not seem to be any real alternative to it.

2. The present wage and salary structure in Britain, however, is not entirely determined by market value, but by various illogical and partly indefensible factors. Even market value is in some respects illogical. For example, because people are prepared to pay considerable sums to be entertained, film stars and boxers have monetary rewards that appear to be out of proportion to the contribution they make to the life of society. Similarly, some trades and professions have a better reward than

their work justifies because they are in a position to "squeeze" the public. Other illogicalities might be described as historical anomalies. The vicar of a rural parish with a hundred or two people may have a large stipend because the lord of the manor happened to be prosperous in the fourteenth century, whereas the vicar of a parish in a new district of a town, with twenty to fifty times as many people to look after, may have a much smaller stipend. In many spheres the inequality due to such anomalies and illogicalities is slight and is being gradually removed in the course of time. The Christian should approve of the ending of such inequality, but he also realizes that to try to do so rapidly might destroy the feeling of security in a wide area.

One sphere where the inequality is more serious is that of industrial and commercial enterprise. The high rewards of successful enterprise are to some extent justified by the market value of the practical wisdom of the *entrepreneurs*. With the coming of large-scale organization the difference to the company or country between a good man and a second-rate one may be thousands or even millions of pounds; but first-rate men are scarce and can therefore demand salaries that are enormous, if they are in salaried work. If sufficiently large salaries are not offered, such men may employ their practical wisdom as private capitalists. It seems, however, that practical wisdom gains higher rewards than are strictly justified by "market value", even in this wide sense of the term. This is because in a changing society enterprising individuals can gain high rewards by taking advantage of novel features in the situation—higher rewards than would be possible in a stable society, or in the same society after the features in question have ceased to be novelties. To some extent, then, the high monetary gains of successful private capitalists at the present time are due to the "historical accident" that we are living in a society which is in process of adjusting itself to technological advances.

The Christian should here support attempts to reduce the rewards of *entrepreneurs* to the genuine market value of their practical wisdom and to remove the excess due to accidents and anomalies. A proviso, however, is that there must be no undue interference with the freedom of individuals, e.g., to employ their talents as private capitalists rather than looking for managerial and administrative posts. In the foreseeable future, managerial and administrative skill is likely to remain scarce and its market value high; and this is a fact that has to be accepted. The reward of the "captain of industry", however, whether employee or independent capitalist, should not be immeasurably greater than that of the Prime Minister. That it should be somewhat greater is not out of place, since the Prime Minister's rewards of a non-monetary kind are greater than those of the industrialist. The most useful contribution of the Christian to this question is an attempt to reach a fair estimate of the relative importance of the work of statesmen and industrialists for the life of society as a whole.

Another activity which, apparently because of historical accidents, receives a reward that is not in accordance with its market value or with its importance for the life of the community is the rearing of children. In this case the reward is less than the market value. The activity of bringing up children is of the highest importance for the community, especially children with high mental and physical endowments. Hitherto the community has relied on the natural impulses of human beings to maintain an adequate supply of children. In recent decades, however, increased facilities for avoiding the conception of children have made the bringing up of children much more a matter of deliberate decision; and the decision has often been made on selfish grounds—if parents limit themselves to one or two children, they will be able to afford a car, and so on. Up till now the tendency to have very small families has been most noticeable in some of the higher strata of society, but it is now to be seen also in sections of the working class. For the community as a whole this is a serious matter except in so far as it is offset by a decline in mortality among infants and children. Since it can no longer be taken for granted that people will produce and rear children, the state in Britain has begun to offer inducements in the form of direct allowances and reductions in income tax, and it seems likely that even greater inducements will have to be given in the near future.

The Christian attitude on this question is based on funda- mental views of the purpose of life. The purpose of mankind as a whole, so far as we are able to understand it, is twofold : to maintain itself in existence and, if possible, extend its life; and, in the course of this, to live nobly. These might be called the biological and ethical ends respectively; and the biological end is primary or substantival, while the ethical end is secondary and adjectival—though in another sense the ethical is higher and subsumes or incorporates the biological. Now society main- tains and extends its life by producing and rearing children. Nearly everything society does is done for the children, to hand on to future generations the material and spiritual heritage we have received. The production of children thus has a more cen- tral place in the life of society than is suggested by most treatises on politics and economics. All our imposing political and eco- nomic organization is for the sake of the children. Consequently any married person who is capable of producing and bringing up children, and who deliberately avoids doing so for selfish reasons, is avoiding a fundamental function in the life of society through which his or her own life becomes meaningful. Simi- larly, for a man or woman deliberately to avoid marriage, except where celibacy is a means to performing some useful and socially desirable function, is to risk having no meaning in one's life. The producing and rearing of children is the most important thing that the great majority of us do with our lives. Successful parenthood certainly has its own—non-monetary—rewards, but it also deserves to be had in honour as a contribution to the life of society and as almost the most important kind of work that is done for society. The Christian will endeavour to see that the work of parenthood is held in greater honour, and will conse- quently support all measures to reduce the financial and other strains of parenthood.

3. Inequality of reward is also connected with questions of

social status. Men want to feel that they are important, and to a great extent they look upon monetary reward as the measure of importance, though some men may be more interested in non-monetary rewards, such as power and public esteem. Much of the desire for higher wages, especially of the desire for differentials, springs from this need to feel important. Frequently the desire for a higher standard of living is not for the comfort or pleasure that it gives, but for the feeling of higher social status. Men want to feel that they are "upsides with" other people, and that they are able to afford what others can afford. With this is bound up the worship of respectability, that is, an undue emphasis on the outward forms of those who are a trifle above oneself socially. This is often accompanied by a tendency to ostentation, for what matters to those who are concerned with social status is not, for example, that they should derive enjoyment from the possession of a piano, but that they should be *known* to possess one.

There is much in this that the Christian, and indeed any moralist, must condemn. All useful and socially desirable work is honourable, and the person who performs such work is therefore leading a meaningful life, and, in the eyes of the Christian at least, has an honoured status in society. In so far, then, as the striving for a higher social position is due to the belief that some useful and socially desirable work is not fully honourable and meaningful, the striving is mistaken. What is true, however, is that men differ in their abilities, their characters and their interests; and some are consequently better suited for one type of work and others for another. Because of this, too, it is justifiable that men should strive, within the field of socially desirable work open to them, to attain to the position in which they will be able to exercise their powers most fully; and in most cases, though not in all, this will mean that men are justified in striving to attain posts with a higher monetary reward. Though such striving for fuller opportunities of work often resembles externally the striving for a higher social status, the difference of motive is great, and a society in which the former kind of striving was dominant would differ considerably from our existing society.

These remarks may be illustrated by considering the contemporary demand for equality of educational opportunity. This demand in fact means that any child, however low the social status of his parents, should be able to obtain a post with a high social status, if he has sufficient intelligence. There is, of course, much justice in this demand, though the attempts to meet it are to some extent warped by the mistaken quest for a "higher" social status. Thus in Britain at the moment it would seem that more people are being given an education to suit them for "white-collar" jobs than there are jobs of this kind in the country, while too little is being done to give men and women an education suited to the conditions and needs of manual workers. Likewise, too much importance is attached to purely intellectual attainments, probably since these can easily be tested by examination, and not enough importance to character, temperament and outlook.

The aim of a national system of education should be to fit all the members of the society to live meaningful lives in the performance of their work. Since many will be workers in industry and agriculture, their education should be relevant to their future life. The difficulty here is that it is not always certain even at fourteen, far less at eleven, what a child is going to do with his or her life. There is much to be said for postponing the decision as late as possible, and for giving all children the same type of education until this decision is made. The latter point is important because a child's attainment at school affects the decision about his work. Nevertheless, it is not in the interests of the nation that its best children in respect of intelligence, character, and outlook should be held back, for the sake of uniformity and impartiality, from special training which would be advantageous for them.

Traditionally an education, which has been supposed to be superior, has been open to the children of parents who could afford to pay fees. In the best examples, this education has really been superior, though in others it has probably been inferior to that provided freely by the state, and has only justified its cost to its patrons by imparting the accent of the "higher" social classes. More recently children have been selected for superior types of education by competitive examinations at eleven plus. This latter course achieves a type of impartiality between the various social strata, but it has disadvantages, and it is probably not in the best interests of the nation as a whole. It fosters the mistaken idea of "rising" in the social scale, and it creates a feeling of anxiety and insecurity in the children. This method of selection is also to some extent failing to achieve its object of securing and training candidates for certain types of important and responsible work. The reason is that selection on the basis of intelligence, or of purely academic attainments, takes no cognisance of other factors, such as character, temperament, and outlook, which are often necessary for the successful performance of important and responsible work. In particular, what I have called "outlook" is largely dependent on the child's family. The son of a cabinet minister, high trade union official, or even industrial magnate, is likely to have a much better understanding of affairs and of the practical working of our social and political institutions than the son of a navvy, even if the two have the same intelligence quotient. What is more widely pertinent is that the preparation for the highest posts in the professions (according to present arrangements) usually requires a man to be content with a very small remuneration for a number of years—until he is twenty-five or thirty—whereas the boy of working-class parents tends to have the outlook that a good wage may be expected before one is twenty. It is more difficult for such a boy than for the son of middle-class parents to be content with scholarships and to apply himself to his studies, when he sees his contemporaries with more money to spend and more leisure to spend it in.

It is futile to say that the son of the cabinet minister has an unfair advantage over the son of the navvy. It is a fact which cannot be circumvented that a child is not simply an isolated individual with a certain intelligence quotient; to a great extent the child is made what he is by his family background. Commonsense therefore indicates that family background should be explicitly taken into account in education. The method of selection by fee-paying is far from perfect, but the best hope for the immediate future would appear to be in some modification of this system in order to ensure that outstanding children whose parents were unable to pay fees should benefit from this superior system of education. Only exceptional children, however, are able to jump several grades "above" the social class of their parents.

The Christian attitude in these matters is to insist on the dignity of all socially useful work, while accepting the fact that children are different. The child ought to be made to see that, whatever its place in school examinations, it is capable of having a meaningful life as a useful member of society. It should be encouraged to make efforts, not to "rise" in the social scale, but to develop its talents and to discover how it may use them most fully with satisfaction to itself and with advantage to society as a whole. These ends, too, should not be lost sight of in drawing up a curriculum.

The question of equal pay for women is another point where social status is relevant. Indeed, the demand that women should receive the same pay as men for the same work is primarily a demand that the essential equality of men and women should be recognized. It is impossible to discuss the history of this matter here, but it may be noticed that some writers have suggested that the idea that women are inferior is largely a consequence of the social changes involved in the industrial revolution. Be that as it may, the present position is that the idea of feminine inferiority has had some popularity, but that the essential equality of women is now generally admitted in theory, and public opinion is now rapidly moving towards an acceptance of the principle of equal pay. The Christian believes in the essential equality of men and women, and therefore supports the movement for equal pay, though without forgetting that other matters are involved, such as the monetary rewards of parent-hood. In the long run the principle of equal pay for equal work should lead to a more economical use of the abilities of men and women, by inducing them to specialize in the kinds of work for which they are most suited.

Another question involving social status is "the flight from domestic service". While the conditions of domestic work may have something to do with this, the feeling that it is menial and inferior work is probably the chief ground for the flight. A charwoman, when she agrees to come to you for a few hours a week, regularly remarks that she is "just doing it to oblige you", although you know that she is eager to have the money. There is clearly a failure to believe in the dignity of all work. Yet the interests of the nation as a whole require that the time of its leading men and women should, as far as possible, be con-served for their primary tasks. No one would expect cabinet ministers regularly to help their wives to dry dishes—though it might not be bad for them to do it occasionally. There are also many other men and women whose time is valuable. There might be some disagreement about when a man's time becomes so valuable that his household should have abundant domestic help, but there should be no disagreement about the principle. It should follow, too, that, where a man is doing important work for the nation, domestic work that eases for him the mechanical business of living is a useful contribution to the life of society.

One way in which the time of important men is conserved is that the company or institution for which they work appoints secretaries, chauffeurs, and other helpers. Because these are ap-pointed and paid by the company or institution, they are able to regard their jobs as contributing to its functioning. Even if it is agreed, however, that cabinet ministers and university vice-chancellors should have adequate domestic help, it does not follow that this should be publicly appointed. Men's needs and tastes vary, and it is therefore found more advantageous to give the man a salary sufficient to provide the necessary help, but to leave the details of spending it to himself. Unfortunately this often leads to a feeling of personal subordination which is regarded as connoting essential inferiority and is resented in a way in which subordination within an institution is not resented. Subordination there certainly is, but it should not imply inferiority. The difficulty is possibly not so great in the case, say, of a cabinet minister, and those who cook his food and wash the dishes should be able to feel that they are making a useful contribution to the life of society and that their lives are meaningful; they should also realize that there are good reasons for not having meals with the cabinet minister, but that, though their work is subordinate to his, they are not essentially inferior as persons. More difficult is the case of the man who is on the border-line of being important, and whose time is far less precious than that of the cabinet minister. It is most difficult when the man's reasons—or his wife's reasons—for wanting domestic help are mainly in the realm of social snobbery and not in order that he may perform his work more efficiently.

In this matter, as in the others where social status is involved, the Christian attitude is to insist on the dignity of all useful and socially desirable work. All such work well done is worthy of respect. In the second place, however, the Christian accepts the fact that men have widely varying abilities, leading them to take up different kinds of work, and that the kind of work to some extent determines his interests and the circle of people he associates with in his free time. A general adoption of the Christian attitude might not affect the structure of the various groups within society, but it would certainly affect the attitude of the various groups to one another, and ultimately the details of their conduct.

The Christian attitude on questions of freedom

It has previously been noted that a certain measure of freedom from authority and from tradition is desirable in a changing society in order to facilitate the adjustments to the new conditions. It appears, however, that West European and American society in the sixth decade of the twentieth century has sufficient freedom of this kind for its immediate needs. The problem before the world is rather that of unification, both of the national societies and of the world society; and in the process of unification a new problem of freedom appears. The mechanization of communications, by making transport more rapid and wireless receivers universal, has created a trend towards uniformity. Nearly all of us listen to the same wireless programmes and read one or two of the same few national newspapers. In so far as this trend towards uniformity promotes the unification of society, it is desirable. But at the same time it leads to dullness and dreariness. Within the growing unity of society, there is therefore a place also for a growing variety and diversity; and this presupposes certain kinds of freedom for self-determination. Above all what is required is the freedom or ability to be oneself, and this belongs to the realm of spirit not of matter. It involves accepting that determination of one's life by society that is socially desirable, but acting independently in other respects. This independent activity, however, must not be a mere reaction to social determination, for such activity is still socially determined. It must be a realization of potentialities of one's own being.

In this connection it is worth noting that money is an important instrument of self-determination. In a society of imperfect beings such as we are, rationing is the only alternative to money as a means of distributing goods and services; and everyone who has experienced it knows how curbing and frustrating the system of rationing is. It leaves the individual practically no choice. He might prefer to spend all his available money on butter and none on tea, or all on tea and none on butter; but the usual rationing system does not permit him to exchange tea coupons for butter coupons. Similarly, if the rationing system was extended, there might be appropriate rations of domestic help for cabinet ministers, vice-chancellors, and other important persons; but, without great flexibility, the ration might be unsuited to a man's special tastes and needs. The desired flexibility is much more easily attained by the use of money. This applies in all spheres, and not only in those mentioned. It applies in the selection of men for jobs. Without money—and the need to earn money to keep oneself and one's family alive—there would have to be direction of labour; and that would mean that our lives were under the dictatorship of petty bureaucrats. The use of money here—the varying of wages in accordance with the attractiveness of the work, its social status, and the number of qualified candidates available—preserves men's freedom.

Though money is thus the instrument of freedom, it is not a perfect instrument. It may happen that some groups of men are in a position to "squeeze" or blackmail others in more or less legal fashion, and that their predatory instincts have to be restrained. Again, the complaint that there is "rationing by price" may sometimes have some justification, namely, where there is gross unfairness in the distribution of the nation's wealth. In a time of emergency, too, it would be wrong if the rich could obtain more than enough of the essentials of life, while the poor starved. In normal times, however, where there is a fair wage and salary structure in a country, with a satisfactory minimum wage, the system of "rationing by price", if one cares to give it that name, leads to a fair distribution of goods and services, in accordance with proper differentials, and at the same time gives men the largest possible measure of freedom.

The ownership of property, especially of one's own house, is to be encouraged because it increases one's self-determination. There is an opportunity for impressing the stamp of one's own personality on what is one's own. Ownership is also to be encouraged on general ethical grounds because, through the responsibilities it involves, it nurtures a more mature character. From the economic standpoint, however, owning one's own house is bad in so far as it makes it more difficult for workers to move from one district to another. On the other hand, such mobility of labour is undesirable from a wider social standpoint, since the constant moving of house tends to reduce people to a dull uniformity and to destroy individuality. The family that is always on the move has no roots in any one local community, through which it may receive definite characteristics other than those of society in general.

With regard to freedom and self-determination, then, the Christian attitude is to support those measures which lead to variety, or rather to the full expression of individuality within a social framework. Variety is not to be sought for variety's sake, but true individual development normally leads to variety; and variety of this sort is essential to the full and abundant life of any society.

Conclusion

After this long discussion of "the application of the cure" to the troubles of a nation, it will be useful to sum up the results and to make some general points that have been implied in the discussion, though not expressly stated.

The cure can only be applied to the troubles of a nation when a sufficiently large number of persons in the nation are not merely nominal Christians, but have responded in some measure to the archetypal synthesis presented in Jesus, and have through this response had psychical energies released. It is not necessary that all the members of the society should be active Christians in this sense; a minority may be sufficient to "leaven the lump".

In so far as men thus respond to the archetypal synthesis and have psychical energies released, they will normally come to exemplify Christian conduct and Christian attitudes in the ordinary personal relationships. A high standard of uprightness is thus assumed, but it is not in itself enough to cure the troubles of the nation. The psychical power that has been released must also be directed towards the transformation of group attitudes. The task of the ordinary Christian who has no special responsibility as a leader is to work for the transformation of his own attitudes. If he is successful in this, he will inevitably influence those with whom he associates. For the Christian leader the task is to examine the group attitudes of the groups to which he belongs in order to discover where they are corrupt and in need of transformation. Then he must struggle with the corrupt attitudes in his own thought and conduct, and he must help others to appreciate the corrupt character of such attitudes. At the same time he must insistently assert the positive corrective principles, such as the dignity of all work that contributes to the good life of society, the share of all workers in the life of society, and the nature of the aims to which the life of society is directed.

4 THE APPLICATION TO THE WORLD SOCIETY

The troubles of the world society are no less than those of the particular national societies, but the consideration of them need not take so long, since the general principles of applying the cure in this field are largely the same as in the particular society. In both fields the troubles arise from group attitudes, that is, attitudes present in the majority of the members of a group and affecting both the personal conduct of the members towards the members of other groups, and also the corporate conduct of the group, through its executive organs, towards other groups. The ideas of security, equality, and freedom may once again serve as pegs on which to hang our considerations.

The physical unification of the world has increased feelings of insecurity. Formerly you could, generally speaking, only be attacked by your near neighbours; nowadays you may be threatened by people who live on the other side of the world. Moreover, the advance of technology has given men new weapons of mass-destruction—though the historian may doubt whether Hiroshima was more horrible than, say, some of the atrocities of the Mongols in the thirteenth century, the former is much nearer to ourselves.

These feelings of insecurity, whether in nations or in smaller bodies politic, lead to a magnifying of the importance of one's own group and a belittling of the importance of other groups. The nomadic Arabs prior to Muhammad illustrate this with their two kinds of poem; in one they "boasted" of the glories of their own tribe and showed how its heroic achievements exemplified the highest human excellence (as they conceived it), while in the other they spoke of the baseness and contemptibility of their enemies. Despite the many differences, modern war propaganda has the same basic pattern. On the one hand it portrays one's own side as superior in various ways—in ideals, in general conduct and in military success; and on the other hand it suggests the inferiority of the enemy—his false ideals, his lower standards of conduct (sometimes amounting to atrocities), and his military failures. As people become more sophisticated, more subtlety is required to induce them to believe in their own superiority and their enemies' inferiority—crude atrocity stories will be dismissed as mere propaganda. The basic needs of average human beings, however, remain the same.

One of the ways in which bodies politic attempt to achieve security is by extending their power and influence. There appears to be in the human make-up a desire for power over other persons, and what is to be said here is not intended to deny this. Nevertheless, there is in groups and in individuals, combining with ambition or the desire for power and also to some extent underlying it, a feeling of inferiority, often largely unconscious. The feeling that Germany, despite her great gifts, had been left behind in the race for colonies had much to do with her two attempts at world conquest. At the present time the Soviet bloc professes, not entirely without justification, to be afraid of the Atlantic Treaty powers, while the Atlantic powers consider themselves menaced by the Soviet bloc. The imperialistic extension of the power of a single country gives a measure of security of a kind. The strong empire is well able to defend itself from the attacks of external enemies. There is internal insecurity, however, in so far as the subordinate groups are disaffected towards the ruling group. The likelihood of such disaffection is greater as the subordinate groups become politically conscious, unless the "empire" has an ideological basis in universal principles. Hitler's essential aim was an imperialistic extension of the power of Germany, but a basic part of the underlying ideology was the belief in the superiority of the ruling group—the Germans as "Herrenvolk", or the Aryans as a superior race. Even if Hitler had been militarily successful, this ideological structure could hardly have supported a world-empire for any length of time. It is improbable, then, if not impossible, that a genuine unification of the world should come about through the imperialistic extension of the power of a single nation or group of nations.

Another way in which bodies politic try to escape from insecurity is by forming alliances. The examples are innumerable. At the present time there are two main alliances in our human society which may for convenience be referred to as the "free world" and the Soviet bloc. There are elements of imperialism in the Soviet bloc, and at least of economic imperialism in the "free world", but these may be neglected here. In these alliances a nation has a measure of security from external dangers which it would not have in isolation. By entering an alliance a nation protects itself from a major threat to its security, but there are also minor threats from the other members of the alliance. The ultimate success of the alliance, therefore, depends to a great extent on its ability to create an area of mutual trust in which the members of the alliance can be certain of fair treatment. For the creation of such an area of trust the actual practice of the stronger members of the group is probably what matters most, but there is also a place for the general acceptance of fair principles to regulate the mutual dealings of members.

The United Nations Organization, like its predecessor the League of Nations, has something of the nature of an alliance, but at the present time its chief function is to provide a meeting-ground where nations can discuss their differences and where a single world opinion may gradually be formed. It is far from being a perfect instrument for these ends, yet it contributes something to the integration of the human society.

In this question of security the Christian is primarily concerned with removing the roots of insecurity, that is, in particular, the insecurity felt by a nation or body politic as such. This feeling of insecurity is reduced in so far as there is a balanced view of the place of human society as a whole in the purposes of God. Against this wide background it is possible to see in better perspective the contribution of each nation to the whole, and to avoid both magnifying it and belittling it. In so far, however, as we are still imperfect and do not feel completely secure in our personal lives, we cannot take a truly balanced view of the function of our own group in world society. The function has to be magnified and glorified if the members of the group are to come near fulfilling the function. If it is not exaggerated, they become dispirited and lose that belief in themselves which is necessary to achievement. We may nowadays deride the ideas connected with the phrase "the white man's burden", and see in them a pompous veneer for sordid economic realities. Yet if these ideas had not been held, things might have been much worse than in fact they were.

In effect the Christian says to himself, "My country is part of a world society. What has it of value to contribute to this world society? Is it making this contribution? If not, why not?" In trying to answer these questions the Christian has the advantage of belonging to the world-wide Christian society. Many Christians have friends within this society belonging to other countries and races, and with these, because of the close ties of religion, they are able to discuss freely the merits and demerits of their countries, and thereby arrive at a truer view of the function of each country in the world society. Ultimately, of course, it is those primarily responsible, that is, the Christians in each nation, who must discover and accept the God-given function of their nation in the world society.

With regard to the particular measures for the unification and integration of our human society, the Christian supports those which are genuinely directed towards this end and which seem to him most likely to achieve it. The details must, of course, be left to the statesmen responsible for the conduct of affairs, and their decisions are to some extent based on the method of trial and error—they have to try things out and see how they work in practice. In respect of general principles, however, a widely held and coherent Christian view could hardly be disregarded by the statesmen, and indeed might be found useful by them.

The equality of nations or bodies politic is rather different from that of individuals. In a sense they all perform the same function. Each body politic is concerned with the good life of its members. Their separateness is due partly to the relatively poor communications of former centuries, and partly to men's failure to achieve integration in larger groups. In another sense bodies politic differ more widely than individuals. They differ in number of members, in geographical advantages, in culture, in degree of mechanization and industrialization, in wealth, and in political stability, and present divisions are not permanent and unalterable. In forming decisions about equality or fairness of treatment these factors cannot be disregarded. In the kind of matters that are considered by the Court of International Justice it is clear that all nations should be treated alike, and that no special favour should be shown to large nations over small ones. On the other hand, U.N.O. recognizes a distinction between great powers and others and gives special privileges to the great powers. This is because, in human society as it is, the great powers have heavier responsibilities in respect of world security; and it would be unrealistic to allow a number of small nations with hardly any responsibility to dictate policy to the great powers. This is an example of the way in which the principles of fair dealing between bodies politic have to be worked out in practice. Some experience is required before agreement is reached about such principles.

Greater equality of wealth between countries is desirable. The policy of promoting such equality has been adopted by the more enlightened leaders of the richer countries as a matter of self-interest. Fortunately or unfortunately, the problem of inequalities of wealth between countries is not one that thrusts itself upon public opinion. As individuals the rich men of the poor countries may be richer than the rich men of the rich countries.

We think of men like ex-King Farouk and the Aga Khan. At the same time, most international contacts are between the upper and middle classes. The Egyptian or Indian peasant does not travel abroad to discover that his standard of living is much lower than that of men doing comparable work in certain other countries. Even the British unskilled labourer, if he realizes that, compared with the Indian who works to produce his tea, he is almost a millionaire, does not usually feel it a matter of great urgency to try to redress this inequality. This isolation of the poorer classes is likely to continue for many decades, though the foreign travel involved in world wars does something to lessen it. To a limited extent the ruling groups who are aware of the inequalities of wealth make use of the point in their propaganda; countries have been classified, for example, as "haves" and "have-nots".

This question of inequality of wealth is likely to become of increasing importance. The Christian will insist that the existing inequality should be greatly reduced. The practical measures for achieving this aim, however, will vary from country to country. In many cases progress will be slow, since a higher standard of living will only be possible through improved agricultural techniques, and these in turn will only work properly where there has been radical social readjustment. Approximate equality is all that should be aimed at, for we cannot strictly compare the standard of living of an Eskimo in Greenland with that of an Arab in the desert. More and more the problem will doubtless become assimilated to that of equality between workers with different functions, such as fishermen and shepherds.

Racial equality may also be considered at this point, though in some cases it is also a problem within a particular society. The Christian is bound to insist on the essential equality of members of all races, since this is explicitly stated in the New Testament. It might be argued that this essential equality of all races does not necessarily involve equal treatment in all respects, since the New Testament, while asserting that the slave and the free man are essentially equal, does not insist on the abolition of slavery. To this argument we might reply as follows. Other things being equal, the abolition of slavery is more in accordance with the Christian conception of the equality of all men. In the Graeco-Roman world, however, slavery was an important part of the social structure, and to attempt to abolish slavery would have led to much greater evils, through the disruption of society, than those involved in the form of slavery then practised. In the question of racial equality, however, there is no comparable social structure involved. In a few countries there may be a social structure in which one race generally has the superior functions and another generally the inferior ones; but such societies are already beginning to change. Moreover, there is a world-wide movement, not by any means restricted to Christians, to recognize the essential equality of all races and to express this in equal treatment. This is fundamental to the United Nations Organization, and is the basis of the practices of diplomats. This being so, the essential equality of all races asserted in the New Testament must in the contemporary world express itself in equality of treatment. There is nothing to be said for the anti-Semitic racial doctrines held by some Germans, and the South African policy of "apartheid" is in much the same position.

The whole world is now being subjected to what may be called Eur-american culture. From the standpoint of Africa and Asia there is little difference between the Marxist and the "democratic" forms of this Eur-american culture. Not merely are its outward forms being adopted, but also much of the intellectual outlook associated in Europe and America with the rise of science and technology. With regard to freedom and self-determination, therefore, an important world problem is how to avoid the "Eur-americanization" of the whole world, and its reduction to a dull monotony. In the interests of world unity, as in the interests of the unity of a particular society, a measure of uniformity is desirable; but in the interests of the good life for mankind a high degree of uniformity is to be resisted.

The intellectual aspects of this problem will be dealt with in the next section. Here we may content ourselves with looking at the conception of the vocation of a nation within the world society. The idea that a nation has something that it does specially well and that this is its distinctive contribution to world society retains the element of particularity, while not denying its relationship to the whole. Moreover, a belief of this kind in a nation's special vocation within the whole reduces its sense of inferiority and its need to exaggerate its importance. The vocation of Britain—to give a very rough example—might be held to be in the exercise of practical wisdom, especially in matters of government and administration. The Briton, and particularly the Englishman, is more aware than most people of the factors in the life of societies that cannot be contained within tidy and logical intellectual systems, but which are of importance in the conduct of affairs. Intellectual systems are certainly necessary in the communication of thought from nation to nation; but the British must leave it to others to formulate these systems. British achievements in experimental science are another aspect of the same vocation. Perhaps the peculiar Scottish contribution, if the philosopher David Hume may be taken as an example, is to give a systematic account of the illogical.

The Christian can help by pondering over this question of national vocation. When a nation realizes that there is something it can do well as a contribution to world society, its sense of inferiority and insecurity decreases.

5 THE APPLICATION TO THE RELIGIOUS COMMUNITY

The corruption of Christendom

The two previous sections have dealt with problems of disunity, disunity in the nation and disunity in the world political society. There is another case of disunity, however, of comparable gravity in its effects on human society, namely, the disunity of Christendom. Indeed, we might go farther and say the disunity of the world religions. There is a sense in which the religious disunity of mankind is an extension of the problem which is exemplified in the disunity of Christendom. This section is to be primarily concerned with the disunity of Christendom, but the solution of this problem is also to some extent the solution of the wider problem. From the present standpoint, however, the disunity of Christendom is, in one respect, the more serious problem. If the Christian faith contains the cure for human troubles, we should expect Christendom to be the instrument for their cure; but how can this be if Christendom itself is in need of cure? If the salt has lost its saltness, is there anything else that can be used to salt it?

The first question to consider is whether the corruption of Christendom is possible. It would seem that the answer must be that some corruption is possible. The New Testament shows how the people of God, who had benefited from his redeeming acts and his revelation of himself under the old covenant, became so corrupt that they required a new covenant. Certainly there are differences between the old covenant and the new; but these do not appear to be of such a kind that those who are beneficiaries from God's activity under the new covenant are immune from corruption, either individually or corporately. They are certainly not immune from corruption as individuals. Confession of sins is a fundamental part of Christian practice, and emphasizes the fact that even those to whom "the cure" has been applied generally continue to be imperfect in certain respects. Saint Paul himself, after great and successful labours for the Christian cause, did not regard a return to corruption as impossible in his own case. If Christian individuals, even the best of them, are not immune from corruption, it can hardly be maintained that Christendom as a whole, or Christendom at its heart, is immune. It is true that a corporate body is more than the individuals than compose it; but, if the whole may sometimes be wiser than the parts, it may also be more foolish or more barbaric. History, too, would seem to show that some-

times there has been disease at the very heart of Christendom
—at least at its official heart. What we are justified in maintaining, however, is that up till now Christendom has recovered
from its diseases to the extent that it has been given to us who
are now alive to appreciate the work of Jesus as the cure, in
essence, of all human troubles.

What has just been asserted on the basis of historical experience is confirmed by theoretical considerations. The root of
human troubles is the sense of isolation and insecurity which
appeared in man as he became conscious of himself as an individual. The cure corrects the tendency to feel isolated and
insecure, but the eradication of the tendency requires a long
course of treatment, and is seldom completed in this life. If
individuals thus remain with traces of the disease in them, is it
likely that the community will be entirely free from disease?

Symptoms of the disease are not difficult to find, both in
Christendom as a whole and in the various fragments of it.
They are similar to the symptoms already noticed in the case of
secular societies. Just as the war propaganda of a secular community emphasizes the inferiority of the enemy and vilifies their
actions, so Christendom disparages its religious enemies, and
the fragments of Christendom disparage one another. The chief
result of religious polemics, even if it is not always the chief
conscious aim, is to strengthen one's own party where it is
weak. Polemics rarely converts the other man, but it supplies
answers to doubts to the waverers among ourselves—and do we
not all have our moments of wavering?

Again, just as secular societies tend to magnify their own
importance and superior character, so religious bodies tend to
exaggerate their own claims. A common view is that "we are
entirely and completely right, and everyone else is wrong".
Unfortunately this claim is made by a great many bodies, and
not more than one can be justified in making it. When made
by a small insignificant sect, such a claim to absolute truth is
merely ludicrous. For the student of comparative religion—or,
should we say, to the modern man of scientific outlook?—the

multiplicity of such mutually exclusive claims creates a presumption that none is fully justified. On the other hand, mere numbers prove nothing in this sphere; Biblical and other history have examples of small unpopular minorities proving in the long run to be right. A heightening of such claims to exclusive truth is perhaps to be seen in doctrines of infallibility, such as the Roman Catholic doctrine of the infallibility of the Pope, and the Protestant doctrine of the infallibility of the Bible. In Islam there is a somewhat similar claim that the community of Muslims, when in agreement, are infallible; this is based on a traditional saying of Muhammad, "My people will never agree on an error".

The disunity of Christendom, then, is due to the imperfection of Christians; and there is a strong presumption that no fragment of Christendom is free from this imperfection and corruption. Because Christians claim that they have in essence the cure for human troubles, the all-too-human trouble of disunity in Christendom is a serious matter for them.

The nature of religious truth

To provide a basis for the discussion of this question, it is desirable at this point to offer some preliminary observations about the nature of religious truth. This will not be a complete exposition of the subject, which is one on which our generation requires to do much thinking. Only those points are mentioned which are relevant to an understanding of the present disunity.

Many of the chief conceptions of religion would popularly be called metaphorical or figurative. They differ, however, from metaphors as commonly understood, namely, as literary graces or ornaments. They belong to the class of what might be called "working" metaphors, for which we have no simple nonmetaphorical substitute. "The Athens of the North" is a fancy way of speaking about Edinburgh; but for the "bulb" which gives us light we have no other simple expression available. Everyone with experience of electrical appliances, however, knows what an electric bulb is, and the fact that this is a second-ary usage of the word does not detract from our understanding of the object. Similarly, in the phrase "the love of God", the word "love" may be said to be used in a secondary or meta-phorical way, but this does not hamper the believer's under-standing of the realities expressed by the phrase. The words "metaphor" and "metaphorical", however, have a connotation of unreality and are best avoided in a religious context; and I would suggest that the secondary character of the words used for religious conceptions might be better expressed by saying that they are "pictures". This would avoid the implication of unreality, since pictures are usually pictures of things or reali-ties. It would also allow for the fragmentary character of re-ligious knowledge and for its apparent contradictions. A picture of a castle may be taken from various directions on the ground, and also from the air. No single picture gives you the castle in its totality; each is restricted to some aspects of it. The pictures differ considerably from one another, too; yet all are pictures of the castle.

This metaphor of the pictures, of course, is only a metaphor, and must not be pressed too far. Yet it helps us to understand some things. The realities with which religion is concerned are much more complex than a castle, and so it is not surprising that there are many different pictures of these realities, and that the differences are so great that many people refuse to believe they are pictures of the same things. Even within Christendom the various fragments have produced vastly different interpre-tations of the achievement of Jesus.

An important example of alternative versions of the same thing occurs in connection with the doctrine of the Trinity. Part of the importance of this is that it is embedded in Christian orthodoxy. The Greek version of the doctrine speaks of one *ousia* and three *hypostaseis*, and the normal Latin translation of this would have been one *essentia* and three *substantiae*; but the orthodox Latin version of the doctrine speaks of something different and even contradictory, namely, one *substantia* and three *personae*. The reason for this difference is that the technical terms involved had different connotations and implications in the two languages. The precise meanings of the terms depended on their whole background in the particular language, both philosophical writings and popular conceptions.

This example further shows us one reason why different bodies describe in different ways what are presumably the same religious realities. The two bodies may differ in the non-religious concepts or categories in terms of which they interpret their experience. Another reason would be difference of interests, and this in turn might depend on differences in the experiences of communities. In different geographical and human environments the chief problem is different. For an island community dependent on fishing the greatest of evils may be stormy weather, whereas an agricultural community in close proximity to wild hill tribes will suffer mainly from human enemies. There seems to be a tendency for a community to interpret all life in terms of the problem that has been central in its experience. In Islam, for example, a prominent place is taken by the ideas of men "going astray" and of God "guiding" them; and these ideas doubtless reflect the experience of a desert community for whom going astray might result in a painful death by thirst.

Consideration of such differences between religious bodies leads us on to appreciate another facet of religious truth, which might be called its "rootedness". Religious truth, where it is effective, has deep roots in the life of a community; it grows out of its soil, as it were. Now, until comparatively recent times, mankind has consisted of a number of societies isolated from one another in varying degrees. This isolation of the societies or communities has been reflected in their religious beliefs. Each religious body has elaborated its beliefs in accordance with its peculiar background of thought and experience. The new generations have been initiated into the whole system of belief and practice of the religious body into which they are born. They come to see everything through the eyes of their religious and secular community. Correspondingly it becomes difficult for them to appreciate the standpoint of members of other religious bodies. The difficulty varies with the degree of isolation. It is very great, for example, in the case of Christians and Muslims, and almost non-existent between certain Protestant sects whose members are in friendly association with one another in secular and even religious affairs. There are, of course, emotional difficulties about appreciating the standpoint of another religious body, owing to the fact that most of us have been impregnated with teaching about the superiority of our own body and the inferiority of other bodies. Even when we have in the main overcome the emotional difficulties, however, there are genuine intellectual difficulties to be overcome; and these are largely due to this phenomenon of "rootedness" coupled with the isolation of the various religious bodies.

Parallel to this rootedness of religious truth in the life of a community is the need for commitment in the individual. It is all very well for the sophisticated man of to-day to acknowledge that there is some truth in all faiths; but this is not a satisfactory basis for living. If religious truth is to be a guide for man in times of crisis it must not merely be held in the forefront of consciousness, but have penetrated deep into the unconscious. This is not likely to happen, however, unless a man commits himself, at least in a general way, to one system of religious truth, and makes this his primary allegiance. This should not exclude acknowledgement of the truth in other religious systems, and there should be readiness to learn from these in so far as their insight is capable of being incorporated into the system of one's primary allegiance. Just because we men are imperfect, however, and not completely free from a sense of insecurity, it is important that we should hold that the religious system of our choice is in some respects superior to others, even if it is only so in the sense of being best for us.

The normal state of a man is one of commitment, explicit or implicit, to a religious system, that is, to the beliefs and practices of a religious body; and this is normally the religious body into which he is born. Occasionally, however, a man has to make a decision whether to remain in the religious body of his birth or to attach himself to another. This happens when a new religious body appears or when there are increased opportunities for contact between members of existing bodies. In such cases there must be at least an implicit belief in the superiority of the system chosen. Some men contrive to avoid a decision and merely drift along; but the fear of commitment is the mark of an unhealthy psychological condition.

The reunion of Christendom

The average Christian in Western Europe and America tends to be myopic in looking at the problem of the reunion of Christendom. He tends to think that the problem of reunion is chiefly one of the reunion of the Protestant sects, or of these with the Anglicans and the Roman Catholics. Yet, from the standpoint of the emerging society it is hardly too much to say that the most serious part of the problem is the gulf between all these on the one hand and the Eastern Orthodox churches on the other. This gulf is all the more serious because it roughly corresponds with that between the Atlantic powers and the Soviet bloc. The chief Orthodox church is the Russian Orthodox Church; and Moscow, as the Third Rome, has inherited some of the hatred of Byzantium for the First Rome. From a world standpoint even the separation of the so-called heretical oriental churches, such as the Coptic, Syrian, and Armenian, is perhaps just as serious as the bickering within Western Christendom, for in a sense these churches are forerunners of the new churches springing up in Asia and Africa.

Let us give further consideration to this last matter. It links up with the discussion of the nature of religious truth. The churches just mentioned, which I call "oriental" to distinguish them from the Eastern or Holy Orthodox Church, used Greek for many official purposes, but they had their roots in communities whose primary language was Coptic, Syriac, or Armenian, and not Greek. With this difference of language went differences in men's whole outlook on life and its problems. As a result the interpretation of the Christian faith in these communities was different from that of Christians whose primary language was Greek. It has already been noted how there were differences between Greek-speaking and Latin-speaking Christians, and how these differences affected the Greek and Latin formulations of the doctrine of the Trinity. Unfortunately the oriental languages were not thought sufficiently important to have their formulations of doctrine acknowledged as valid by the oecumenical councils where they differed linguistically from the Greek and Latin formulations.

This is exactly the problem that is likely again to become serious for Christendom during the next few generations. The new churches in Asia and Africa necessarily adopt to begin with the forms of belief and practice of their parent churches. As they reach maturity, however, and their roots go deeper into the life of their communities, their interpretation of the Christian faith will be more and more in accordance with their own background of thought and experience. The Christian faith will come to be at home in Tamil and Swahili as well as in Greek, Latin, and English; and when the Tamil and Swahili formulations of Christian doctrine are translated back into English and Latin, they may well shock English-speaking and Latin-using Christians. When this happens, will the leaders of Christendom have more wisdom than those in the early centuries who made heretics of Copts, Syrians, and Armenians?

This is the heart of the world society's problem of unifying many particular traditions and yet avoiding a dull uniformity. Christian leaders must encourage the linguistic and geographical subdivisions of Christendom to retain their particularity; and yet this particularity may come to endanger the unity of Christendom. The solution of the problem will require wise and large-hearted statesmanship in all the various cases. One important principle seems to be provided by the Greek and Latin trinitarian terms, namely, that there should be a readiness to acknowledge assertions in different languages as equivalent, even where they are not linguistically identical. Where expressions are thus acknowledged as equivalent, though they are actually different, it is assumed that they will be used with tact and mutual consideration. There must be a "gentleman's agreement" not to "tread on other people's corns". The Greek must not develop his conception of three *hypotaseis* in such a way that it appears to be a denial of the one *substantia* in Latin.

This possibility of one religious body denying (or appearing to deny) some aspect of the beliefs of another religious body, which the latter regards as fundamental, is not a mere academic supposition, but the source of most religious disputes. In Western Christendom the liberal who accepts the results of higher criticism in general is felt by the fundamentalist to endanger the authority of the Bible, which is the very centre of the fundamentalist's belief; while to the liberal the fundamentalist's denial of the general validity of higher criticism endangers the principle, which is very important for all liberals, of the unity of all truth, both religious and scientific.

An instructive example of how one religious body may come to deny something essential to the faith of another is the Islamic denial that Jesus died on the cross. There is a reference to the matter in the Qur'ān (4. 157/156) in a passage refuting the Jewish claim to have killed Jesus; it was probably implied in the claim that, because Jesus was thus killed, he could not have been a prophet. The words of the Qur'ān are vague, but the main point is clear: "they did not kill him and did not crucify him, but he was counterfeited for them". A somewhat similar belief had already been held by Gnostic Christians. With the Muslims the underlying thought presumably was that God would not allow a man whom he had sent as a prophet to be overcome by his enemies. Now this is a belief which may be said to have been held by Christians also. It is not far from the thought in a verse of the Psalms which was quoted by the apostles: "Thou wilt not suffer Thy Holy One to see corruption" (Acts 2. 27; Ps. 16. 10). Thus, because Muslims believed something which Christians also believed, the Muslims came to

deny the crucifixion where the first Christians had asserted the
resurrection. The difference is to be ascribed to the different
contexts of thought and experience in which the belief was
operating. This relatedness of origin, of course, does not make
the denial any less serious. The Muslim denial of the crucifixion
threatens an essential point of the archetypal synthesis of Christianity. In this particular case the threat is not formidable in
practice, since the bare Qur'ānic denial, even if it was widely
known by Christians, would not avail against the circumstantial
details of the gospel narratives.

These differences of background have not merely led in the
past to the break up of a unity (and may do so again in the
future); they are a serious obstacle to the reunion of Christendom at the present time. The improvement of communications
is reducing such differences, but they will continue to be relevant to religious disputes for many generations. With this discussion of differences in mind let us turn to questions of reunion.

There are two main conceptions of how reunion may be
brought about. One of these conceptions is that associated with
the Ecumenical Movement and the world Council of Churches,
and exemplified in the Church of South India. The other conception is that of the Roman Church. The Roman conception is
that the doctrinal and institutional framework of unity already
exists in the Roman Catholic Church, and that reunion comes
about by acceptance of the doctrine and incorporation in the institutional system. The Roman conception has led to an impressive measure of unity over a large area. Its weakness is that it is
unable to make much allowance for differences of background.
Differences of liturgical form and institutional detail are per-
mitted in the case of the uniate churches; but there appears to be
little readiness to permit the spontaneous development of doctrinal formulations in any linguistic and intellectual context
alien to the Latin one. Such developments require a freedom of
mind that is not fostered by the discipline of the Roman system.

The other conception is of reunion through compromise. The
various bodies that unite, or contemplate uniting, try to distin-

guish between the essentials and the non-essentials in the beliefs of each, and then to find a statement of the essentials which will be acceptable to all. The danger here is that in zeal for unity a religious body may regard as non-essential, and so abandon, some facet of its archetypal synthesis which was really indispensable to its continuing vitality. This danger is a real one since these religious bodies have often come into being largely in order to emphasize their distinctive beliefs, and have derived their vitality mainly from these beliefs. On the other hand, the danger is lessened where the distinctive beliefs refer to issues that were alive two or three centuries, but are now dead.

Among the adherents of both conceptions part of the motive for seeking unity is the feeling of inferiority and the desire for greater strength. Rome sees the strength of a large disciplined body. The Ecumenical Movement sees the increase of strength that would come if the fragments of Christendom were joined together. Conversely both are aware of their weakness in the face of a partly hostile world, and are moved by this. Thus the urge to unity proceeds, at least in part, from man's imperfection. It does not follow, of course, that it is wrong to seek unity; but the striving for unity must be critically examined. Religious leaders must certainly do all they can to strengthen the bodies for which they are responsible. Strength does not come from mere numbers, however, nor from a vast organization. It would seem that there is even a point beyond which doctrinal unity does not contribute to strength. Strength comes from the effective operation of an archetypal synthesis, inducing men to respond to it and, in the measure in which they respond, releasing psychical energy.

From this it follows that the particular steps taken to maintain or extend doctrinal and institutional unity cannot in themselves bring about an increase of religious or psychical strength. They can at most create conditions which make it possible for this strength to increase and which tend to prevent its decrease. What a religious body regards as heresy is thus seen to be what hinders men's response to its archetypal synthesis. Where there is a large community consisting of several distinct groups, such as Christendom was in the fifth and sixth centuries, it is difficult to find doctrinal formulations which satisfy every group. What satisfied the Christians who spoke Greek and Latin did not satisfy those who spoke Coptic, Syriac, and Armenian. The same trouble was probably present in the schism between east and west and in the reformation. At the present day the question is coming to the fore whether what is satisfactory for European and American Christians is satisfactory for Bantus and Chinese. Thus doctrinal uniformity promotes strength only up to a certain point; beyond that point it leads to weakness in so far as it stifles the response to the archetypal synthesis in some sections of the religious body.

On the other hand, institutional unification without an adequate basis of doctrinal unity may endanger men's response to the archetypal synthesis just as much. It must constantly remain difficult for ecclesiastical statesmen to know whether to be intransigent over a certain point or to compromise by admitting the identity of linguistically different formulations. The decision in any particular case ought to depend on which course appears likely to make possible the fuller response to the archetypal synthesis.

The individual's contribution

When the individual Christian realizes that there is imperfection and corruption in Christendom, he naturally asks, "Is there anything I can do about this?" It is difficult, however, to do anything, for he himself is involved in the imperfection and corruption. Moreover, to try to escape from his involvement in corruption by denying his allegiance to the religious body to which he belongs does not help matters. Religious truth is only effective when a man is committed to one system of religious truth. There are occasions when a man is justified in changing his allegiance. There are occasions when a man is justified in working for the union of religious bodies which he regards as approximately equal. There is no justification, however, for being without definite allegiance and commitment to any religious body. When this need for commitment is acknowledged, the following lines of activity seem to be open to the individual Christian, and, indeed, to the individual adherent of any of the great world-religions.

With regard to his own religious body, the individual ought to aim at understanding and appreciating its position more fully, and at conducting his life more in accordance with its teachings. If he comes to see that in some respects the claims which it makes are exaggerated, yet in other respects he may discover that it has a latent strength of which he had not dreamt. In this way he will be doing something to lessen the feeling of inferiority in himself and his co-religionists, and so to weaken the tendency to make exaggerated claims. Exaggeration is unnecessary in so far as men are aware of the true basis of strength. Moreover, when a man's life is in accordance with his religious profession, he is contributing to the religious unification of the world. His life is something public, which affects other people, including members of other religious bodies. If it is a good life, the latter are impressed and hold in respect both the man and the religious body to which he belongs; and respect for other religious bodies is an important condition of unity.

With regard to other religious bodies, the attitude to be adopted by the individual is more complex. We are usually farther from the truth in our criticisms of other bodies than in our exaggerated claims for our own bodies. Even when we are convinced that our criticisms are true, we must be moderate in expressing them publicly, remembering the dominical injunction, "Judge not, that ye be not judged". Even this is not enough, however. We must cultivate the humility of spirit that is ready to learn from other religious bodies, while remaining loyal to our own. It is not inconsistent, for example, for a Muslim, while holding that Islam is superior to all other religions, to adapt to Islamic needs Christian methods of giving religious instruction to children or explaining the faith to unbelievers.

In much the same way a Christian may find in another Christian body an emphasis which is lacking in his own, and he may be able to incorporate this emphasis into his own system without radical changes.

The individual, then, while remaining faithful to the light which he has received within the religious body to which he owes allegiance, is to be always open to whatever religious truth is presented to him by the lives of those with whom he is in contact. One of the features of the contemporary world is that contacts between members of different religious bodies are closer and more numerous. Men are seeing at first hand the "fruits" of other religious bodies, that is, the type of lives they produce. These ' fruits" of religious belief in human living are in a sense the work of God, operating through the Divine truth contained in the religious beliefs of the various bodies. Openness to Divine truth is thus complementary to a readiness to acknowledge valuable "fruits" wherever they may be. In some cases a man will be able to incorporate into his own set of beliefs the truth that he sees in another religious body. There will also be many cases in the modern world, however, where a man is not able to incorporate fresh truth, but has to face a decision about changing his religious allegiance. In general it is probably wrong for an outsider to try to hasten such a decision, though there may be cases where it is helpful to a man to be "pushed" a little by an outsider. There is certainly a place for the presentation of religious truth by convinced believers to any who will listen. Most changes of allegiance, however, will probably be brought about by exposure to the "fruits" of another religious body.

There are two further things to be said. One is that it aids us in preserving openness of mind if we remember that our supreme aim is to serve God and not to preserve our religious body. Mostly God wants men to serve him by remaining loyal to the religious body in which they were born, but sometimes he places them in circumstances where they cannot truly serve him without abandoning their religious allegiance for another.

The second thing to be said is that everyone who honestly

tries to be faithful to the light and truth God has given him is contributing to the fulfilment of God's purposes. At the present time we cannot tell when or how God is going to bring about the unity of Christendom or of all mankind. As Christians we believe that in Christ is the cure for all human troubles; we think it likely, too, that there will be a great outburst of psychical energy, perhaps before the end of this century; but we cannot say what precise form of the Christian archetypal synthesis will lead to this outburst. What we know, however, is that those who are faithful to their light are making their contribution, and that their lives are meaningful.

It may seem that there is little the individual can do about remedying religious disunity. This is in fact the case. The individual man is not God, but only God's creature. In the sphere of mankind's religious life, even more than in those of its political life, national or global, it is reserved to God to create unity.

4

PHILOSOPHICAL REFLECTIONS
ON THE CURE

WITH HIS sense of weakness and inferiority man is distressed by any appearance of incoherence in his religious beliefs. One of the procedures he adopts to defend himself, therefore, is to reduce his religious beliefs as far as possible to a coherent system. The attempt to give a systematic intellectual account of the achievement of Jesus and what was presupposed in it led the Church to the doctrines of the Incarnation and the Trinity. It is popularly thought that these doctrines are much too subtle and mysterious for the ordinary man to understand; but in my opinion this is a mistaken view. Admittedly, there are many subtleties in the theological discussions of these doctrines in the early centuries; but these subtleties, I should maintain, are in large part due to the different intellectual backgrounds of the various groups of Christians. When these historical discussions are left aside, and the doctrines are expounded in terms of the conception of the universe held by our contemporaries, it should be possible for the ordinary educated man to comprehend at least the outlines of the doctrines. It is such an exposition that is attempted in this chapter, and it presupposes as basis the views put forward in my book, *The Reality of God* (S.P.C.K., 1957).

I THE CLAIMS OF JESUS

General considerations

Before anything can be said about the claims of Jesus it is

necessary to adopt some attitude with regard to the authenticity of the New Testament record. Here I can do no more than state the attitude I adopt. To give the reasons for it would lead too far afield.

The four gospels give four pictures of Jesus. The pictures are slightly different from one another; and the differences are to be ascribed to the different conceptions of Jesus held by the evangelists or their sources. This has suggested to some modern scholars that the gospels distort the figure of Jesus; and on this supposition they have attempted to elicit factual details from the gospels by critical methods, and from these factual details to build an undistorted picture of Jesus. Such a procedure I hold to be based on false epistemological conceptions. In the gospels the picture of Jesus in the mind of the evangelists controls the presentation of the details, and it is not now possible in many cases to abstract details from the record as a whole, and regard them as absolutely objective. The evangelists did not distinguish as we do between literal and metaphorical truth (or should we rather say "between material and spiritual truth"?). Consequently, in some cases no answer is possible to modern questions about the objectivity of details; and we have to acknowledge the limits to our knowledge. This is humbling to our intellectual pride, but not a serious practical drawback.

The primary question about the truth of the gospels thus becomes whether the pictures in the minds of the evangelists were true pictures of Jesus. To this question I would give an unqualified affirmative. These are pictures of Jesus, perhaps not in his inner nature, but at least as he appeared to men. If these pictures are not true, then we have no picture of Jesus, and no means of obtaining any. The slight differences between the pictures do not prove their falsity. They are what we would expect from four writers of different temperaments and backgrounds. This means that the pictures are complementary and tend to confirm one another. It should be remembered, too, that the pictures are not simply the individual records of the evangelists.

The gospels grow out of the pictures of Jesus held by the Church or sections of it, and their acceptance by the early Church after they were written further confirms that they corresponded to the orally transmitted picture of Jesus.

The particular application of these points to the question of the claims of Jesus is that the claim to be more than man is such an integral part of all the four pictures of him that it is unthinkable that he did not in fact make it. I would go so far as to maintain that, at least in this respect, the Fourth Gospel gives the best picture of him. In a literal and material sense he may not have uttered every word as it is recorded in the Fourth Gospel; but the Fourth Gospel conveys to us better than the others the gist of his addresses and debates, and what was implied in them. The Fourth Gospel thus illuminates much that is obscure in the other gospels, and in this respect is of superior historicity. In this connection it is worth noting that the conception of Jesus as the Word or Logos is presented, not as a claim made by Jesus, but as the view of the evangelist and the Church.

I adopt the position, then, that the claims which Jesus is presented in the gospels as making were really made by him, and that no evangelist nor any group of Christians would have had the temerity to invent such claims.

The claim to be Messiah

The claim to be the Messiah or Deliverer expected by the Jews is omnipresent in the gospels, and is implicit where it is not explicit. It is implicit in all that is said about the kingdom of God being at hand. It is implicit in Jesus' references to being sent. The Old Testament conception of the Messiah, however, had many facets. That which was uppermost in popular thought in the time of Jesus was the idea of a military leader who would defeat the Romans, and he had to be careful not to be regarded as Messiah in this sense. His concern was in fact to effect such a deliverance of God's people from their enemies as has been described in this book as "the cure in essence of human troubles".

The Messiah had usually been thought of as a human leader. Even the first three gospels, however, depict Jesus drawing his opponents' attention to the fact that the Messiah is not merely a human being. In the Temple during the last week he quoted Psalm 110:

> The Lord said to my Lord, Sit thou on my right hand, till I make thine enemies thy footstool.

He called attention to the words "my Lord", which were commonly taken to refer to the Messiah, and showed that they implied that the Messiah was somehow superior to David (Mark 12. 35-37 and parallels). The very title "son of man", which Jesus is depicted as using regularly of himself, has more than human implications. A passage in the book of Daniel describes the more-than-human activities of the "son of man"; and, with reminiscences of this passage, Jesus is reported to have said to the people:

> And then shall they see the Son of man coming in the clouds with great power and glory. And then shall he send his angels, and shall gather together his elect from the four winds . . . (Mark 13. 26 f.).

It is most significant that, in a reply of Jesus to the high priest, there is a reference to both the Old Testament passages mentioned.

> Again the high priest asked him, and said unto him, Art thou the Christ, the Son of the Blessed? And Jesus said, I am: and ye shall see the Son of man sitting on the right hand of power, and coming in the clouds of heaven. (Mark 14. 61 f.).

Finally, we may notice a verse in the first two gospels which suggests that, while the angels are above men, "the Son" is above the angels.

> But of that day and that hour knoweth no man, no, not the angels which are in heaven, neither the Son, but the Father (Mark 13. 32).

"The Son" here presumably means the "Son of man", who has been mentioned a verse or two earlier; but, since there is also a reference to the Father, this forms the transition to a discussion of Jesus' claim to sonship.

Jesus' claim to be Messiah is thus depicted as involving a claim to be more than human. This latter aspect was present in some of the Old Testament conceptions of the Messiah, though in a vague form. According to the first three gospels Jesus did little to remove the vagueness and to develop the point, but he certainly called attention to it and included it in his claims.

The title of "son"

Jesus is apparently never depicted as saying in so many words, "I am the son of God". This may have been to avoid the semblance of arrogance in this form of words, or it may have been to avoid misunderstanding. He certainly made the claim indirectly, speaking of himself as "the Son" and as being in a special relationship to the Father. Moreover, when other people used the phrase of him he approved of it and did not deny it. When Peter at Caesarea Philippi confessed "Thou art the Christ (or Messiah), the Son of the living God" (Matt. 16. 13-17), he welcomed this as precious insight given to Peter by the Father. Similarly, when referring to an accusation of blasphemy on the ground that he had claimed to be God's son, he does not deny that he had made the claim (John 10. 36-8). The words "because I said, I am the son of God" would naturally be taken as implying that he had in fact said this, but they might perhaps also be interpreted as meaning "because (as you allege) I said . . ."; thus the fact that Jesus did not deny that he had made the claim is more conclusive. It should be noticed, too, that the Greek words in this passage (unlike those in Peter's confession) are best translated "I am God's son", and do not permit us to say with certainty whether this means "*the* Son of God" or "*a* son of God".

The claim to sonship has an Old Testament background. God

frequently speaks of the people of Israel as his son, and also applies the name to David and to his promised seed. The name is not commonly applied to the Messiah, but it occurs in Psalm 2. 7, "the Lord hath said unto me, Thou art my son; this day have I begotten thee". Jesus must have been aware of this passage. There is a reminiscence of it in the voice which spoke to him at his baptism and to the three disciples at his transfiguration (Mark 1. 11; 9. 7; and parallels). From the conception of sonship it was natural to pass to that of fatherhood. Even in a passage about the Son of man we find a reference to "his father".

> Whosoever therefore shall be ashamed of me . . . of him also shall the Son of man be ashamed, when he cometh in the glory of his Father with the holy angels (Mark 8. 38).

Thus Jesus made a claim to Divine sonship, and this claim was in some sense a development of Old Testament ideas. The claim to sonship, too, was bound up with a claim to stand in a unique relationship to the Father. The idea of sonship by itself, however, is seen to be inadequate as an expression of the unique position of Jesus. Israel as a whole is often spoken of in the Old Testament as God's son; and, though this indicated a unique relationship which Jesus in a sense inherited, his own relationship to the Father was closer. He himself quotes a verse from the Psalms (82. 6):

> I have said, Ye are gods; and all of you are children of the most High.

This, he points out, implies that those to whom the word of God came could be called "gods" (John 10. 34 f.). Indeed, an earlier passage in the same gospel (John 8. 33 ff.) depicts the Jews as claiming to be sons of God. In the course of a discussion of the true nature of freedom the Jews introduced the argument that they were free because they were the descendants of Abraham; in reply Jesus suggested that they were servants of sin and children of the devil.

> I speak that which I have seen with my Father: and ye do that which ye have seen with your father. They answered and said

unto him, Abraham is our father. Jesus saith unto them, If ye were Abraham's children, ye would do the works of Abraham. Ye do the deeds of your father. Then said they to him, We be not born of fornication; we have one father, even God. Jesus said unto them, If God were your Father, ye would love me . . . Ye are of your father the devil.

Thus the term "sons of God" or "children of God" was apparently not unknown to the contemporaries of Jesus; and he seems to have been concerned to show when it might properly be applied. It occurs occasionally in his reported sayings.

> Blessed are the peacemakers: for they shall be called the children of God (Matt. 5. 9).
> But love ye your enemies . . . and ye shall be the children of the Highest: for he is kind unto the unthankful and to the evil (Luke 6. 35, cf. Matt. 5. 45).

It is therefore not surprising that the conception of "sons of God" was prominent in the thought of the early Christians. It seems to have been much more prominent among them than it is among the Christians of to-day. Two quotations may suffice.

> As many as are led by the Spirit of God, they are the sons of God (Rom. 8. 14).
> As many as received him, to them gave he power to become the sons of God, even to them that believe on his name: which were born, not of blood, nor of the will of the flesh, nor of the will of man, but of God (John 1. 12).

Despite the prominence of this conception, and despite even such passages as that where St Paul speaks of Jesus as "the firstborn among many brethren" (Rom. 8. 9), the Christians of New Testament times did not confuse their own sonship with that of Jesus. They knew that his was primary or original and that theirs was secondary or dependent. This was sometimes expressed by saying that the Christians were "sons by adoption".

Thus it was appropriate that Jesus should claim to be God's son because of the place that the conception of sonship had had in Jewish thought. The claim does not, of course, imply physical sonship, but is a claim to stand in a unique relationship to the Father. To understand the precise nature of this relationship, however, we must leave aside the word "son", since it is not without ambiguities, and consider some of the other ways in which Jesus is reported to have expressed this relationship. St John will be found the best guide in this respect, and three main points may be made.

Firstly, the activity of Jesus is the activity of God.

> My Father worketh hitherto and I work . . . The Son can do nothing of himself, but what he seeth the Father do: for what things soever he doeth, these also doeth the Son likewise (John 5. 17 ff.).

This theme is present throughout the Fourth Gospel. It must be kept in mind when we are contemplating Jesus' claims to be the bread of life, the light of the world, the good shepherd, and the way, the truth and the life. To feed and so to sustain life, to illuminate, to protect and deliver from evil, are Divine activities. Jesus therefore performed operations which were recognized as being within the sphere of God's activity.

Secondly, Jesus has a unique knowledge of God's nature and of his purposes for mankind, and this he shares with men. St Paul, in comparing the Christians with sons as contrasted with slaves or servants, makes this knowledge of God's purposes a distinctive feature of the sons. The germ of the thought seems to be contained in a saying of Jesus recorded by St John.

> Henceforth I call you not servants; for the servant knoweth not what his lord doeth: but I have called you friends; for all things that I have heard of my Father I have made known unto you (John 15. 15).

The claim to unique knowledge of the Father also appears in the First and Third Gospels.

> All things are delivered unto me of my Father: and no man knoweth the Son, but the Father; neither knoweth any man the

Father, save the Son, and he to whomsoever the Son will reveal him (Matt. 11. 27; cf. Luke 10. 22).

Thirdly, Jesus claims that his is in some sense one with the Father.

I and my Father are one (John 10. 30).
He that hath seen me hath seen the Father . . . Believe me that I am in the Father, and the Father in me (John 14. 9, 11).

We see, then, that the phrase "the son of God", while appropriate to denote the unique relationship of Jesus to the Father, in view of the background of Jewish thought, does not give a complete account of that relationship. Still less are we likely to understand the relationship by studying the connotations of the word "son" in modern English. Let us seek a fuller understanding by attempting to describe the relationship on the basis of the scheme outlined in *The Reality of God*.

There are two main questions which require an answer. The first of these concerns the relationship of Jesus to the Father and will be considered sufficiently in the next section. The second question is how we are to conceive Jesus as both God and man, and that may be considered here as the culmination of the study of sonship.

Christians insist that Jesus is truly human. In his humanity, however, he is completely responsive to God. In this respect he differs in degree from the mass of mankind, even the saintliest of them. This complete responsiveness is to be ascribed to the absence in Jesus of the bad effects found in men as a result of their growth into self-consciousness; that is to say, Jesus had no undue feeling of weakness and inferiority. The experience of the agony in the garden, however, and the experiences lying behind the cry of dereliction on the Cross, show that Jesus had a genuine human self-consciousness. Yet in being conscious of himself as an individual, he did not cease to be aware of his oneness with humanity and the rest of creation, and of the close dependence of creation on the Creator. The experiences of loneliness, however bitter, were transitory, and did not destroy the union of his will with that of the Father. Still less, of course, had feelings of separation any part in determining the set of his will.

Of the three above-mentioned aspects of the unique relationship of Jesus to the Father—Divine activity, Divine knowledge and unity—the knowledge of God's nature and purposes is the positive side of the absence of the bad effects of becoming self-conscious. This means further that Jesus could consciously co-operate with the Father in the achieving of the Father's will in the world. In so far, however, as all that human beings do is in a sense done by God, and in so far as many men learn to submit themselves to God's will and to co-operate with him, the conscious co-operation of Jesus with the Father is not a mark of his uniqueness. The special nature of the work he achieved has also to be taken into account, that is, the cure in essence of all human troubles; as St Paul put it, "God was in Christ reconciling the world unto Himself" (2 Cor. 5. 19). The work of Jesus was a special Divine activity appropriate to the central crisis of human history. Moreover, it involved the presentation of God to men in archetypal form, capable of evoking a deep response from them. Thus it was not in some matter of detail, but in fundamental Divine activity that Jesus was consciously co-operating with the Father; and in living out the archetype he was in an important sense one with the Father.

2 GOD AS THREEFOLD

The orthodox Christian faith is that God, though truly and genuinely one, is also in some sense threefold. This belief was forced upon Christians by their experience of Jesus and his achievement. There was a second experience, or set of experiences, however, that led them to insist that the Holy Spirit was also a hypostasis in the Godhead.

The kernel of the experience of the Holy Spirit was what happened on the day of Pentecost, a few weeks after the death and resurrection of Jesus. That may be described as an outburst of psychical energy following upon Jesus' presentation in his actions of an archetypal synthesis. Those in whom psychical energy was released were cured of their troubles. Their characters became stronger and more integrated. Contrast the timidity of Peter which led him on Good Friday to deny his association with Jesus and the boldness with which, not long afterwards, he defied threats of arrest and went on preaching. This was the primary experience of the Holy Spirit, and it was shared by all the first Christians. Subsequently they came to ascribe also to the Holy Spirit the conceiving of Jesus in Mary's womb and the revelations to the prophets of the Old Testament.

Such, then, is the functioning of the Holy Spirit as it has been experienced and observed. The Holy Spirit, however, is a hypostasis of God; and we have adopted the position that God is the supreme principle of integration in the universe. How is the Holy Spirit to be described in terms of this position? As a provisional account we might suggest the statement that the Holy Spirit is the supreme principle of integration in its immanent operation within groups and individuals. This requires amplification and qualification, however. One question that immediately presents itself is whether, in every case where psychical energy is integrative in its effect, we are to recognize the working of the Holy Spirit. Most Christian theologians would probably answer this question in the affirmative; but they would distinguish a general or universal activity of the Holy Spirit from a special activity in God's people. To the universal activity of the Holy Spirit would be ascribed not merely the integration effected in men and in human society but also that which we may observe in the lower creation. Correspondingly the distinctive feature of the special activity of the Holy Spirit in the Church would be that this activity is concerned with overcoming the disintegration caused by the appearance of self-consciousness. With this and other refinements, however, the above statement would seem to be satisfactory for a preliminary understanding of the Holy Spirit.

The achievement of Jesus is also in a sense an immanent activity of the supreme principle of integration. How, then, is Jesus related to the Holy Spirit? It was maintained in the previous section that the uniqueness of Jesus lay in his living out an archetype or, more exactly, an archetypal synthesis. According to Christian teaching the Holy Spirit was active in preparing the archetype in his life, suffering, death, and resurrection. The archetype, in its historical presentation, however, is distinct from the immanent activity of the principle of integration leading to the presentation. If we may use the phrase "material form" in a wide sense to include a series of historical events, then we may say that archetypes are material forms and that by the contemplation of these material forms men are able to become sufficiently aware of the transcendence of God to make a response to it. This account is intended to apply to all archetypes in all religions, even those which are polytheistic and those which seem to deny God altogether. In the eyes of the Christian, of course, the archetypal synthesis of Christianity is superior to the others. It is because the life of Jesus is archetypal that as God the Son, the second hypostasis of God, he is distinct from the Holy Spirit.

It is comparatively easy to indicate the experiences in which the second and third hypostasis are found, but the case of the first hypostasis is more difficult. What experience corresponds to the Father? One might be inclined to say that it was the experience of the Jewish people in the Old Testament; but this would be wrong. Christian thinkers soon realized that, though recognition of the threefold nature of God followed upon certain experiences, God must have been threefold from all eternity. Thus the experience of the Old Testament was not specially related to the Father, but rather to God conceived wholly or mainly without differentiation of hypostases. The experience corresponding to the Father must therefore be looked for elsewhere. In line with what has been said about the Holy Spirit the statement may be offered that the Father is the supreme principle of integration in its transcendence, that is, as beyond and above the created universe. The corresponding experience is the awareness which sometimes comes to men of a meaning, a significance, a value, which transcends space and time, and which cannot be destroyed by the death of the individual or the species. This is doubtless the experience which the Bible describes as "seeing the glory of God".

This is a very brief outline of the most profound question with which the human mind can deal. Its aim is to do no more than open up a line of thought. If what has been said is sound, then we see dimly how the supreme principle of integration is three-fold. It is transcendent; it has an immanent integrative activity which is known chiefly from its effects; and it has an immanent activity of an archetypal character. These are what the Greeks called the three hypostases of God. At the present time the Greek *hypostasis* is perhaps less misleading than the anglicized Latin "person". The word *hypostasis* means something like "distinct thing" or "distinct object of awareness". In the experience of the working of the Holy Spirit in the Church, in contacts, direct or indirect, with the historical events of the life of Jesus, and in the vision of the glory of God, we are aware of three distinct things. That is to say, as they present themselves to us, and as we are first aware of them, they are distinct; but reflection forces us to hold that they are ultimately one. In an account of the being of God such as has been given here the danger is that the unity of God will be emphasized at the expense of his threefoldness; but what has been said about the meaning of *hypostasis* is perhaps sufficient to show that a reasonable account can be given of the distinction between the *hypostases*.

In offering these philosophical reflections my chief hope has been to convince open-minded persons that the doctrines of the Incarnation and the Trinity are not mere pieces of obscurantism, but attempts—and indeed successful attempts—to give a reasoned and systematic account of what is implied in the achievement of Jesus. They are not easy to understand; but the difficulty in understanding them is of the same order as, say, understanding the nature of man. Some degree of understanding of them should be possible for anyone who is capable of following a philosophical discussion. One of the great needs of our time is for a profounder appreciation of the reality of God; and for those who have been brought up in the Christian tradition this appreciation cannot be separated from some understanding of his threefoldness.